Heaven in your Eye, Earth on your Heart

—a taste of Boston, Baxter
and Bunyan for the journey

by Steve Donald

EP BOOKS
Faverdale North
Darlington
DL3 0PH, England

web: http://www.epbooks.org

e-mail: sales@epbooks.org

EP Books are distributed in the USA by:
JPL Distribution
3741 Linden Avenue Southeast
Grand Rapids, MI 49548
E-mail: orders@jpldistribution.com
Tel: 877.683.6935

British Library Cataloguing in Publication Data available

ISBN 978-1-78397-040-7

Whatever the future holds, the great writings of the puritans can give us inspiring and practical help for our passage through these troubling times for the church. Steve Donald takes us on a fascinating journey with some of the giants of that heroic age, who kept heaven in their sights throughout their tumultuous lives and ministries on earth.

Lee Gatiss, Director of Church Society and editor of *Pilgrims, Warriors, and Servants: Puritan Wisdom for Today's Church*

Martin Luther said; 'There are only two days in my diary, today and that day.' Luther's desire was to live every day in the light of the fact that one day he would stand before Christ. Steve Donald's book will help us all to understand both the encouragement and challenge of living in this way.

Peter Maiden, International Director Emeritus Operation Mobilisation

Contents

Preface by Philip Hacking

'So heavenly minded, no earthly use' was a criticism levelled at enthusiastic Christians in my formative years. Too often the reverse would now be true.

Steve Donald draws out the biblical principles which enabled seventeenth-century evangelical leaders to make an impact in their generation and serve as examples to challenge us today. Many who share their view of biblical authority face similar attacks from the secular world and the often-compromised church of today.

These examples of 'radical discipleship' and 'passionate spirituality' should stir up modern Puritans, not ashamed of their often-despised title, sadly seen as negative rather than painfully positive.

Here is a call to individual Christians to maintain their concern for holy living and to pastors and church leaders to stand up and be counted.

The word 'Christian' is once more in the public domain with many nuances. Let us not be ashamed of it and find in these stories a new inspiration to be prepared for the cost.

'looking to Jesus, the founder and perfecter of our faith, who for the joy that was set before him endured the cross, despising the shame' (Hebrews 12:2)

Folk to thank for the book

Personal

To my wife Gloria my best encourager.

To my daughters Lizzie and Abi and my son-in-law Ben. I especially dedicate this book to my infant grandson Reuben. May he grow up to love the Puritans.

To Rev. David Craven who gave helpful criticism but also encouraged me in the early stages and Dr Dan Berkeley who looked through the first draft and gave me encouragement to carry on. To fellow ministers both Anglican and non-conformist who gave me such encouragement to keep going on with the book.

A special word of thanks goes to Moray Henderson who helped edit the book and made many helpful comments along the way.

Authors

I've been helped by many authors and I've tried to give credit for their work in the book. For the chapters on Thomas Boston, Philip Ryken was particularly helpful. For the English Puritans, J. I. Packer, especially his lectures at Reformed Theological Seminary, were very useful. You can access them free of charge on:

http://itunes.rts.edu/rss.html

1

What's your sailboat?

In the popular children's bestseller, *A Series of Unfortunate Events*, by Lemony Snicket, a little family who had been through a continuous set of cruel circumstances conclude that 'to have each other in the midst of their unfortunate lives felt like having a sailboat in the middle of a hurricane'.[1] Just after my family and I went through such a storm, my younger daughter drew us a picture, which I still have in my study, of each of us, holding hands and dancing and smiling, with the sun shining over us and the quotation from the children's book at the top of the picture. She wrote on the bottom of the picture, 'Whatever happens we have each other!' She was right that our family had been brought closer, but what really mattered was God's love that glued us together and enabled us to become better not bitter, in spite of our suffering. Christian friends also played a crucial role, helping us to interpret this experience through the lens of God's love; but it was very difficult, and we still have the bruises several years on.

The Christian life is tough and we need to be prepared for that reality, rather than think as many do today, that becoming a Christian will give us a more comfortable life on earth while we wait for heaven. It won't. In fact, it may well make life much more difficult for us. What we need, which I believe the Puritans can help us with, are the means of flourishing in the midst of painful struggle. Dallas Willard in his influential book, *Renovation of the Heart* writes,

> A carefully cultivated heart will, assisted by the grace of God, foresee, forestall, or transform most of the painful situations before which others stand like helpless children saying 'Why?'[2]

The Puritans can help us form this cultivated heart. At our wedding in 1984, the vicar told us in the introduction to his sermon what he had read in his diary that day: 'Some people bring happiness *wherever* they go, whilst others bring happiness *whenever* they go!' Of course we all want to be the 'joy-bringers', but life is always a mixture of pain and pleasure, of bad news and good. How can we build a carefully cultivated heart so that we can spiritually thrive in the good and the bad times we all go through? That is the subject of this book. Interested? The Puritans lived in times of angst like ours, but had a cheerfulness, godliness and effectiveness far beyond our own. They can provide rich resources for the journey to heaven, whilst keeping our feet very firmly on the earth. They can teach us to have heaven in our eye and earth on our heart.

Whatever happened to heaven?

When was the last time you heard someone talk about their hope of heaven, or listened to a sermon on heaven? The popular writer C. S. Lewis understood that a daily vision of heaven has the potential to transform our lives on earth. He also saw that heaven does not figure much in our thinking in modern times. Lewis thought this was one reason for our lack of effectiveness in the world as Christians.

> Hope is one of the Theological virtues. This means that a continual looking forward to the eternal world, is not (as some modern people think), a form of escapism or wishful thinking, but one of the things a Christian is meant to do. It does not mean that we are to leave the present world as it is. If you read history you will find that the Christians who did most for the present world were just those who thought most of the next ... It is since Christians have largely ceased to think of the other world that they have become so ineffective in this. Aim at heaven and you will get earth 'thrown in': aim at earth and you will get neither.[3]

Lewis's list of Christians empowered by a vision of heaven could well have included the Puritans, who accomplished a lot on earth as they daily meditated on 'heaven's joys'. They found this emphasis on heaven in the Bible. Abraham, for example, is described with the other Old Testament saints, as 'a stranger and exile on earth'. Such folk are pilgrims, who 'desire a better country, that is, a heavenly one' (Hebrews 11:13, 16). Paul writes of the Christian pilgrimage on earth as, 'we look ... to the things that are unseen. For the things that are seen are transient, but the things that are unseen are eternal' (2 Corinthians 4:18). The Lord Jesus himself speaks often about the nearness of eternity: 'In my Father's house are many rooms. If it were not so, would I have told you that I go to prepare a place for you?' (John 14:2). In Matthew 18:10, Jesus says, 'See that you do not despise one of these little ones. For I tell you that in heaven their angels always see the face of my Father who is in heaven'. The Christian apprentice's prayer begins: 'Our Father, in heaven'. Given the importance of heaven in the Bible, it is surprising how little heaven features in our day to day thinking and living. It is the contention of this book that the destination must shape the journey.

Why choose the Puritans?

Puritans like Thomas Boston, Richard Baxter and John Bunyan found that meditating daily on the glory to come empowered their devotion to God and made them more effective on earth. When I read Dallas Willard's *Renovation of the Heart*, it raised within me lots of questions about what form this renovation of my heart might take. I happened to pick up Richard Baxter's *The Saints' Everlasting Rest* and it got me thinking about the Puritans and the impact of heaven on their lives. From there I read again Bunyan's classic *Pilgrim's Progress* and then discovered Thomas Boston, who penned the eighteenth-century *Human Nature in its Fourfold State*, a synthesis of Reformation and Puritan thought. Through my study of their writings I have discovered a secure sailboat for these troubled stormy days. These three godly men have given me a solid vessel upon which to continue my spiritual journey through life. They have put into my hand precious resources to continue the journey with renewed hope, faith and love. I am writing this book to share something of that experience of renewal and recommitment, with the desire that it may help others going through the occasional hurricane, the more usual choppy waters and the precious calm of the Christian life.

Another motivation for writing was my son-in-law's love of the Puritans and his recent call to full-time paid ministry in the Church of England. Many Reformed Anglicans are asking: 'Is there a long term future for us in the Church of England, given the moves towards women bishops and the growing acceptance of homosexual practice amongst the clergy?' Perhaps we might face in the future something like the 1662 ejection of two thousand godly Puritans from the Church of England? Whatever the future holds, and whatever pressures in our lives, we need resources to keep us sailing on faithfully, until we reach the safe haven of heaven. The Puritans can give us help that is both inspiring and practical. Evangelicals in non-conformist churches are facing the same pressures in different forms and would benefit from a study of the Puritans view of heaven as well.

A good example is Boston's *The Crook in the Lot* a meditation on the godly response to trials based on Ecclesiastes 7:13, 'Consider what God has done: who can straighten what he has made crooked?' The Christian's arrival in heaven is underpinned by the goodness, providence and sovereignty of God. Boston says that, 'There is not anything whatever befalls us without his overruling hand'.[4] 'It is God who makes the blind, the poor, the barren and the deaf. It is impossible for us to make straight what God has made crooked. As we submit to him even trials can be a source of blessing to our souls'. This biblical outlook to the adverse circumstances of our lives has the potential to transform them and give us that cultivated heart able to rise above trials rather than be pulled down by them. According to Boston, God has a reason behind the crooked providences of life that can be a source of blessing.

Amongst his list of seven examples he includes 'excitation to duty, weaning one from this world, and prompting him to look after the happiness of the other world.'[5] Another Puritan concerned about God's providence was Obadiah Sedgwick, who wrote, 'The church is like a ship at sea, endangered by waves and winds; but divine providence sits at the helm, powerfully guiding and preserving it'.[6]

A Puritan Mind

In the first section of this book the sailboat or raft will picture the biblical paradigm for salvation as expressed in Thomas Boston's *Fourfold State*. A paradigm is something that serves as a pattern or model. Ultimately it is the gospel (Romans 1:16) that gets us to heaven but Boston's theological construct is a faithful expression of it that has helped many to a greater understanding of the gospel. The sailboat is not the cultivated heart. This is a by-product of joining the crew of this vessel (the Church), which helps us spiritually thrive in adverse circumstances. The Puritan Richard Sibbes, known as 'the heavenly doctor Sibbes', in the seventeenth century wrote about the comfort Christ gives to his servants undergoing trials in his book *The Smoking Flax and the Bruised Reed* and comments that their [the apostles'] comfort grew with their troubles'.[7] If we are honest, for most of us, unlike the apostles (and many of the Puritans), our comforts decrease in direct proportion to our trials! Boston's *Fourfold State* will give us a sailboat of biblical thinking that will help us to put our trials in context.

In this book, I want to present three distinctive traits of the Puritans as shepherd, soldier and pilgrim, which will demonstrate that they 'aimed at heaven and got earth thrown

in', to use C. S. Lewis' point. Thomas Boston best exemplifies
the shepherd, whilst Richard Baxter and John Bunyan, who
both served in Cromwell's army, are the epitome of the
soldier-pilgrim. We will also look more briefly at a fourth
man, William Gurnall, author of *The Christian In Complete
Armour* who, whilst clearly a Puritan, decided to accept the
infamous Act of Uniformity that led to the ejection of two
thousand godly Puritans, including Richard Baxter. My thesis
is that all four men show the paradoxical nature of the Puritans,
who had this twin vision of heaven in their eye and earth
on their heart. Both aspects were important but heaven was
dominant. This was something quite basic to the Puritans and
by looking at their covenant theology and the main features
of Puritan thought through the eyes of these men, I will seek
to show that this vision of heaven was of central importance
to their world view. In Section One we will test this thesis by
examining Thomas Boston, described by Philip Ryken as 'the
last of the Scottish Puritans and the first of the Evangelicals in
Scotland'.[8] In section Two, we will look more closely at three
English Puritans caught up in the controversy of 1662, and then
conclude with an examination of how heaven was at the heart
of their writing and living.

All of this will have the aim of putting the doctrine of heaven
into practice, what a later Christian leader, Martyn Lloyd-Jones,
who gained a lot from a study of the Puritans, called 'Logic on
fire'.[9] The Puritans were committed not only to sound theology,
but to a doctrine for life. With this sailboat or raft we can
develop '*a carefully cultivated heart, assisted by the grace of God*',[10]
so that we can better navigate our way to the haven of heaven
through stormy and difficult waters. My earnest prayer is that

this might be as great an encouragement for you in the journey as it has been for me and countless others.

Section 1
The Shepherd-Captain

2

Thomas Boston (1676–1732)
Shepherd-Captain

Why should we read Boston today?

We need a raft of salvation

Growing up in the north-east of England in a small mining village by the North Sea, my brother Jim and I had a wonderful 'ready made' playground close to a timber yard near the local coal mine. We spent many happy hours during the summer holidays, building rafts from the timber and floating them on the nearby pond. I've always liked the story of Noah building his ark, to preserve him and his family from God's judgment expressed by the flood. Of course, when Jim and I built rafts we only used logs lashed together with bits of rope, whilst Noah built an ark 450 feet long, 75 feet wide and 45 feet high, made of cypress wood and coated with pitch, with three floors, rooms, a roof on top and a door on the side. The rafts Jim and I made were of very simple construction, but were able to float. As Christians we need a raft to enable us to float on the turbulent waters of modern life. Such a raft, made up of the big picture of the Bible, will give us a place of security.

In the U.K., the Church of England, along with other mainline denominations, is imploding and facing gradual but seemingly inexorable collapse. Whilst it has been a broad church it has been home to a sizeable number of growing gospel-minded churches but its steady departure from Scripture is undermining its attractiveness. In the past it had an agreed agenda based on the Bible, whilst being comprehensive on church order. Now it has become comprehensive on doctrine. Unity appears to be more important than biblical truth. This slide towards liberalism is also true of other denominations like the Baptists and the Methodists. What are evangelicals to do in this situation? Should we follow the exodus to the Church of Rome in order to find a place where we feel secure? Not at all! Rome has serious doctrinal errors that mean no Bible Christian could feel comfortable within her fold. What is wrong with Rome? Papal supremacy, transubstantiation in the mass, Mariology and prayer to the saints are some of her doctrinal errors. Where then shall we go? We must look to our evangelical heritage together with our Free Church friends and like-minded folk in other mainline denominations, because this provides us with a raft to navigate these stormy and uncertain times. We will find in Thomas Boston the sort of shepherd-captain we need; someone who will guide us safely to heaven, but also someone who will help us to make a positive impact on earth.

In the *Iliad* and the *Odyssey* of ancient Greece, ship's captains are called 'shepherds of ships'. A controversial environmental action group have named their ships 'Sea Shepherds'. The idea of a pastor (a shepherd) being the captain of a ship has also gained some currency in contemporary Christian literature. Ruben Exantus writes, 'as the captain of the ship, the competent pastor must be able to steer the church in both good and bad times effortlessly and confidently without wavering emotionally' (*What a tall order!*).[11] Some ministers in the Church of England are called 'rectors', a term originating from the Middle English 'rectour' meaning a *helmsman*. Just as a shepherd guides, protects and feeds his flock as he leads them to safety, so the captain of a boat or ship or even a humble raft tries to do the same. Since I have never yet met a shepherd, (even though I live in Cumbria) and I would guess most of my readers have not done so either, I will use the analogy of the pastor being a captain or helmsman. Thomas Boston is a great shepherd-captain of souls. Through his theological paradigm expressed in his book *Human Nature in its Fourfold State*, he offers us a raft of security on which to travel to heaven. Boston's vision of heaven is so dominant that for him the destination must shape the journey.

For most people today the journey of life is everything, with little thought about what might come after death. They are lost in the journey as I was as a young man. When I was eighteen years old and training to be a physical education teacher in Liverpool, one of my lecturers gave me a significant insight into my life, which under the direction of the Holy Spirit helped me become a Christian. I was struggling to master practical gymnastics to a satisfactory level. Her insight was that I was trying far too hard. I was focusing, she gently told me, so much on achieving the movement that I was making a complete mess of it. This insight helped transform my gymnastic ability to an acceptable level but also suggested to me that my personal happiness was not to be gained by self-effort, no matter how energetically I pursued it. Looking back with the benefit of many years experience it seems so self-evident since 'happiness' is so dependent upon 'happenings' which we cannot control. The first insight people need is to 'take their foot off the pedal' from the pace of modern life, and think.

The second insight is to become self-forgetful. All my life I seem to have had a good *'forgetory'*, having to write everything down in my diary but now I'm in my late fifties I still forget even when I have written things down! But I'm not thinking about that sort of self-forgetfulness. Jesus told us not to pursue personal happiness on this earth with hundred per cent effort, rather that such blessing was to be found indirectly, not by seeking to satisfy self but by the self-forgetfulness of 'seeking first his Kingdom' and by 'taking up our cross' and 'dying to self'. C. S. Lewis, as we saw in chapter one, points to the same paradox when describing the tension between heaven and earth. Lewis said, 'Aim at heaven and you will get earth "thrown in": aim at earth and you will get neither.' If we make earth dominant in the tension between heaven and earth we will lose both. This is what many people are doing today, both inside and outside the Church. They live for themselves and for this world with only a vague sense, if at all, of an eternal destiny. Jesus reminds us in Mark 8:34–36 of the need for self-forgetfulness.

And calling the crowd to him with his disciples, he said to them, 'If anyone would come after me, let him deny himself and take up his cross and follow me. For whoever would save his life will lose it, but whoever loses his life for my sake and the gospel's will save it. For what does it profit a man to gain the whole world and forfeit his soul?'

The third insight is to think about the transitory nature of life and how everything we treasure seems to turn to dust. The hymn 'Abide with me', which I've sung at many funerals, has this evaluation of life on earth:

Swift to its close
Ebbs out life's little day;
Earth's joys grow dim,
Its glories pass away;
Change and decay in all around I see.[12]

When our two daughters were about five and six years old we gave them a bottle of bubbles each to play with. They held the thin plastic stick and blew through the hole. We watched as the red, blue and green bubbles rose into the air. Then they ran after them and tried to catch them in their hands. As soon as they reached for them they popped. An anonymous poem puts it like this,

I'm forever blowing bubbles, pretty bubbles in the air,
They fly so high, nearly reach the sky,
Then like my dreams they fade and die.

We need a raft focused on the eternal world

The final line of the stanza from the hymn 'Abide with me' that I omitted above sums up Thomas Boston's focus: 'O thou who changest not, abide with me'. For Boston and the people of his generation the transitory nature of life was much more apparent since the average life expectancy was around thirty-three! Boston was to bury two of his own children. Death was 'on their shoulder' and the subject could not be avoided. In our culture where life expectancy is soaring, death is a taboo subject, even for Christians. We kid ourselves that the 'good life' will go on forever but it will not and all of us will face death. Hebrews 9:27 says solemnly but realistically in the King James Bible that Boston would have used:

> And as it is appointed unto men once to die, but after this the judgment.

In his preaching and in his writing Boston speaks to this harsh reality so evident to his people and about which so many people today are in complete denial. When I was a member of a church in Lancaster they nicknamed me 'the megaphone', since with my big voice and P.E. teacher background I was useful in making public announcements, even to a large group. C. S. Lewis calls suffering God's megaphone to get our attention and in Boston's day they suffered a lot and life was very hard. Out in Africa today the situation is very similar. On a recent visit to Nairobi I met many Christians who were materially poor but spiritually rich. During two visits to the Ukraine in the mid 1990s I found the same thing. Back here in the U.K. we are generally (when compared to folk in these places) materially rich but spiritually poor as our spiritual senses are dulled by comfortable lives and a National Health Service.

Boston's world echoes that of many Christians overseas.

Together they have much to teach us about spiritual realities. Philip Graham Ryken in *Thomas Boston as Preacher of the Fourfold State,* looks at Boston from the perspective of his preaching and sees this eternal focus as critical to Boston's worldview.

> The proportions of the Fourfold State indicate the importance of eschatological themes throughout Boston's sermons, where the present spiritual condition of the hearer is invariably placed against the backdrop of eternity. As he preaches in 'A View of This and The Other World' (V 299–362) 'Our main concern lies in the world to come' (V 390).[13] [Eschatology is the study of the end times].

Here we see the impact that 'heaven in your eye' makes on Thomas Boston. Heaven is dominant. The eternal state claims a disproportionate part of the 'Fourfold State' since two-fifths of the book covers this subject. He gives, unlike many of his sources, a sustained treatment of both heaven and hell. The effect is to fix heaven or hell very strongly in the minds of his readers as their final destination. The destination must shape the journey. Boston's book spoke in language ordinary folk could understand that made them aware of these realities. His raft not only helped them to see their perilous situation was that they were in a state of sin but also led them to the Saviour and built them up with truth from the Scriptures so they were ready to enter this eternal world.

To say that his book was a phenomenal success was no exaggeration. '*Fourfold State*', was *the most published book* in the eighteenth century, with more than a hundred editions in Scotland, England and America! Jonathan Edwards called Boston 'a great divine' whilst John Wesley said his works were required reading for the serious believer. Boston was a shepherd who led and fed his flock. Not just his small congregation of ninety in Scotland where he laboured, but thousands of folk were blessed through his books. For a generation after his death keen Christians had two books in their home; Bunyan's *Pilgrims Progress* and Boston's *Fourfold State*.

Boston's genius was to build his world view on the best of Reformation and Puritan thought, making it accessible to the ordinary person. Boston's understanding of human nature in its fourfold state was influenced and was in full harmony with the subject discussed in Chapter IX of the Westminster Confession of Faith (1647): *Man in a state of innocence* (IX, 2), *Man in a fallen and sinful state* (IX, 3), *Man in a state of grace* (IX, 4), and *Man in a state of glory* (IX, 5). These form the four 'planks' of our imaginary raft. Boston's book, 'Human Nature in its Fourfold State', gives us a clear picture of covenant or federal theology. By looking at this book and his autobiography, we will be able to investigate the place that 'heaven in your eye and earth on your heart' has within Puritan thinking and living.

Boston followed where others had led. It was Augustine who started thinking about man in paradise and then man in his lost state after the Fall. In the Middle Ages, Peter Lombard's *Sentences* developed the idea of a big picture, which starts with the Trinity in Book I, then moves on to creation in Book II, looks at Jesus the saviour of the fallen creation in Book III, and considers the sacraments which mediate Christ's grace in Book IV. Luther and Calvin read Lombard's Sentences and developed a more biblically accurate big picture of salvation history. Boston then took these ideas and popularised them for the ordinary person.

Ryken writes that 'the "fourfold state" to which Boston refers is a theological construct of noble lineage, sired by Augustine and propagated first to Peter Lombard and his commentators, then ultimately to the theologians of Reformed orthodoxy'.[14]

Are you persuaded?

Perhaps I can end my introduction as to why we should read Boston today by anticipating a couple of objections and then finishing the chapter with a final flourish to get your taste buds going!

Objection 1: The Puritans are 'too heavenly minded to be of earthly use'.

Or to put it another way: 'If the Puritans had this twin vision of heaven and earth, surely one view must dominate to the exclusion of the other?'

At first sight Calvin (and the Puritans were Calvinists) seems to stress heaven to the exclusion of all thoughts of earth when he says,

> If heaven is our homeland, what else is the earth but a place of exile? If departure from the world is entry into life, what else is the world but a sepulchre? No one has made progress in the school of Christ who does not joyfully await the day of death and final resurrection.[15]

If heaven fills the horizon so that *'earth becomes a place of exile'* (Calvin's words) and as a consequence the Christian is not engaged with life on earth then this must be a disaster. This was the weakness of much of medieval monasticism. Did it affect the Reformers and the Puritans in the same way? With Calvin, as with some other writers, he will make an extreme statement and then elsewhere you find a balancing statement. So, for example elsewhere he speaks of legitimate earthly pursuits and concerns. He is no ascetic. When I was a student at Capernwray Bible School, Principal Billy Strachan, who was a former music hall entertainer, used the same approach, except with humour! Just as you were laughing at his exaggerated point he would slip in a balancing statement. Balance is crucial for a right understanding of the relationship between heaven and earth. We will soon discover that Boston's paradigm gives us a vessel of security to keep us straight on the way to heaven, *whilst encouraging us to make earth* a *better* place. It will help create that 'cultivated heart', which gives a resilience to keep going through the storms of life and arrive at our heavenly destination with joyful anticipation.

Objection 2: The Puritans are too hard to read.

There is some truth in this as you will readily agree if you have ever tried to read the Puritan John Owen! Owen is a great thinker but he likes to use a lot of long words. I find that I can just about understand him by reading each sentence out loud two or three times. It's like mining for gold. Well worth the intense effort but requiring a lot of energy and time. If you are just embarking on the Puritans (and there seems to be a bit of a resurgence of interest) then I suggest you start with Thomas Boston; he writes simply for ordinary people like you and me!

A final flourish!

During the time I was writing this book, I spoke about it to a local church's men's group. I wanted to be as practical as possible so I actually built a mock-up version of Boston's 'raft' to explain what the book was about. I went into our vicarage garden and found some thin branches which I then cut into four 'trunks' representing Boston's four states of man. 'Just imagine yourself marooned on a desert island', I said to myself, 'and how you would survive by building a raft from timber on the island'. Anyone who knows me could not picture me surviving beyond a day! I then lashed my 'timber' together with five bits of 'rope' (coloured wool actually), each representing one of the distinctive facets Puritan expert J. I. Packer terms as the five key features of Puritan belief. I inserted another thin branch though a gap between the 'logs', bent to fit inside the 'ropes' so that it would stand erect and secured a horizontal 'mast' (made from an ice lolly stick) with an elastic band which had 'Jesus' written on it in bold black letters. It is Christ who makes salvation possible through his death and resurrection. He, of course, is the real shepherd-captain of our souls and folk like Boston simply serve as under-shepherds for his sheep.

I was very proud of my mock-up raft since I am usually hopeless at craft and DIY! What I haven't confessed is that my 'ropes' were not strong enough to hold my raft together so I had to cheat and nail another couple of ice lolly sticks underneath the vessel to make it hold together. Anyway, I hope you get the idea as the men at the church group did that like Boston my intentions are practical and not just theoretical! Its doctrine for life that we need and Boston is full of it!

Years ago when we were on holiday in France we did not find the way the French cook their meat very appetizing. When you go into an English restaurant and they ask you, 'How do you want your steak?' (if you can afford it these days!), and you reply, 'I'd like it *very rare* please', that will give you an idea of the French idea of cooking meat, with lots of blood! So the Donald family were struggling in their journey through France to find meat that we considered edible. One morning as we travelled through a small town in the south of France I did something I thought I would never do. I punched the air with intense joy when I saw the tall tell-tale yellow sign of MacDonald's in the near distance. Although it was very early in the morning it was open and I soon demolished a 'Big Mac'. If I can put it this way: for evangelicals struggling in the current stormy waters of our culture of narcissism (excessive love or admiration of the self) and egalitarianism (presently characterized by belief in equality for all without reference to God's truth revealed in the Scriptures), the sight of Boston's raft will be like a starving Englishman in France finding and devouring a 'Big Mac'! Oh joy!

3

Who was Thomas Boston and what shaped his life?

In the last chapter I mentioned my boyhood memories of building and sailing rafts with my brother Jim. Ten years later, on leave from the army, Jim invited me to crew for him on a hired dinghy on Windermere in the Lake District. The experience was very unpleasant. Several times we almost capsized and when we brought the dinghy back we had the embarrassment of colliding with the jetty right in front of the owner! Jim confessed recently that when we went out in the dinghy on Windermere he didn't know a thing about sailing! But Boston is the competent shepherd-captain. He knows how to sail the vessel! Boston's eye is constantly fixed on the haven of heaven but he is also vigilant about potential rocks that might be a threat to the voyage on earth. Before looking at the ropes that held Boston's raft together we need to ask about what shaped Boston into such an effective shepherd and captain of men.

On the Banner of Truth cover to *Memoirs of Thomas Boston* it
says of Boston that he was,

> Born in relative obscurity in 1676 in Duns, Berwickshire,
> Thomas Boston died in 1732 in the small parish of Ettrick in
> the Scottish borders. But his 56 years of life, 45 of them spent in
> conscious Christian discipleship, lend credibility to the spiritual
> principle that it is not where a Christian serves, but what quality
> of service he renders, that really counts.

This quotation suggests a man deeply concerned for the
fate of others. He has both heaven in his eye and earth on his
heart. He knows that to focus on heaven (choosing to work in
relative obscurity) is to get earth thrown in and to major on this
transitory world is to lose both. We will consider him first as a
man, then as an author and conclude with Boston's passion for
mission and for the poor.

Boston the man

Thomas Boston was the youngest of seven children. His
father, John Boston, was a cooper (barrel-maker) and a strict
Presbyterian. One of Thomas' childhood memories was visiting
his father in prison, where he had been sent for refusing to
fit in with changes in worship forced on the Scots by the
Stuart kings. Thomas spent at least one night sleeping in the
prison with his father[16] which clearly made a big impression
on him. 'Being a nonconformist during the time of Prelacy,
he suffered upon that head, to imprisonment and despoiling
of his goods.'[17] Relief came in 1687, when non-conformist
Presbyterians gained permission to have services in the houses
of private individuals. John Boston took his family four miles

away to hear Henry Erskine, the father of the well-known Erskine brothers, Ebenezer and Ralph. Thomas records in his autobiography that he came to saving faith aged eleven, while hearing the messages from John 1:29 and Matthew 3:7 that Henry Erskine gave.[18] Boston was shaped by the religious persecution of the day and in his autobiography he often wonders whether he is going to face the same trials as his father or share the ministerial pressures of the Erskines, ejected in 1662 due to the pernicious Act of Uniformity. Alongside such pressures Boston suffered from a melancholy temperament. He writes in his autobiography, 'I am habitually cast down, and cannot win to get my heart lifted up in the ways of the Lord'.[19]

Thomas Boston is most famous for *Fourfold State*, but he also penned *The Crook in the Lot*, a short book noted for its originality, and his *Body of Divinity* and *Miscellanies*. These works had a great influence for good over the Scottish peasantry. In his autobiography published in 1776, he speaks of his many spiritual struggles, the dry spells he went through, his own deep sense of unworthiness and the deadness he felt regularly in his spirit, even when in the process of preaching in church or praying in his study. So here was a man who was open and honest about his failings and struggles, but a man whom God used to reach many thousands of people with the gospel, particularly through his writing. I know someone just like that who, whilst being very talented, has worked in mainly small church situations, in difficult urban parishes and having retired through ill health brought on by his faithful ministry has written nine books that God has used to reach many. So I can picture what sort of man Thomas Boston was, a man like my friend, pastorally warm with a gift of preaching and writing that

ignites devotion to Christ with a heart for ordinary people to
come to Christ and become strong disciples. A man with his eye
on heaven and his heart on earth.

Boston the author

The Methodist W. E. Sangster tells of the preacher who *read
himself full, thought himself clear, and prayed himself hot*; Sangster
concludes that to read, to think and to pray is the only way to
become a preacher in any century. This conviction is echoed by
Boston when he writes,

> I took myself to my studies as soon as I could. Experience of
> this kind hath been one thing, which all along, and especially
> in later years, hath recommended close study to me, and in a
> manner bound it upon me, as being that on which much of my
> peace and comfort depended.[20]

Great writers are usually great readers! The problem for
Boston was his poverty. He owned only a small shelf of books
but he compensated by borrowing many books from his
Christian friends in the pastoral ministry. As he *read himself
full* with as much Puritan material as he could, Boston *thought
himself clear*. His writing was an expression of the desire to
think clearly so that he could preach effectively. His passion for
the gospel meant that *he prayed himself hot* and this resulted in a
deep concern for the souls of others and their circumstances on
earth.

In his introduction to *The Fourfold State* Boston quotes
Ecclesiastes 7:29, which says, 'This alone I found, that God

made man upright, but they have sought out many schemes'. And then he writes:

> There are four things very necessary to be known by all that would see heaven; first, what man was in the state of innocence, as God made him. Secondly, what he is in the state of corrupt nature, as he hath unmade himself. Thirdly, what he must be in the state of grace, as created in Christ Jesus unto good works, if ever he be made a partaker of the inheritance of the saints in light. And, lastly, what he shall be in his eternal state, as made by the Judge of all, either perfectly happy, or completely miserable, and that forever.[21]

In his book Boston gives us the four planks of his raft of security with the claim that these 'four things are very necessary to be known by all who would see heaven'. The pastor of the church is like the captain of a ship who must give a clear direction to his flock. H. J. Westing, in his *Church Staff Handbook* uses the analogy of a ship. 'The senior pastor is a captain, determining priorities and essentials for emphasis, time, and other resources. As a pilot, he or she must steer and coordinate.'[22]

I have been inspired by the clear direction that Boston gives both by his example recorded in his autobiography and by *The Fourfold State*, which gives a biblical framework for a sense of security in a fast changing world. Leland Ryken, writes that 'Like Nicodemus, who was a teacher in Israel but did not know about the New Birth, evangelical Protestants tend to be strangers to what is best in their own tradition.'[23] Writers like Boston can put us back in touch with our evangelical heritage,

and the raft of the big picture of the Bible that can give us
assurance and strength for today's uncertain and stormy waters
and help deliver *that cultivated heart, assisted by the grace of God*
that Dallas Willard writes about.

This fourfold big picture not only gives us a raft of security
but motivation to keep going. We are on a journey to the
celestial city. History is moving not in a cyclical, meaningless
fashion, but in way that has a beginning, middle and end. With
this clear and vivid expression of the gospel in *The Fourfold State*
we have a bold explanation of the state of man and of the world
we live in and an understanding of how the gospel gathers a
people for God's own possession. D. L. Moody said, 'Heaven
is a prepared place for a prepared people'. We live our lives in
preparation for eternity where Christ waits to welcome us. At
the beginning of the Farewell Discourse in John's gospel, Jesus
speaks about his going away so that he can prepare a place for
the disciples so that he can come back and take them to be
with him in heaven (John 14:3). The whole of the disciples'
remaining time on earth is put in the perspective of Jesus' final
return to take them to heaven. 'This interim is bounded by a
future that is determinative for the whole road that they have
to travel. Their life on earth finds its direction, goal, and power
in their belonging to him who is in heaven.'[24] This is New
Testament thinking expressed by Puritans like Thomas Boston,
whose lives on earth are energized by their vision of heaven.
One weakness of the Puritans was a lack of emphasis on the
Second Coming and we will see this later on when we consider
Pilgrim's Progress where this important doctrine is not a feature
of Pilgrim's journey. However, the Puritans have a lot to teach

us about keeping the priority of heaven in our eye and earth on our heart.

Augustine and then Peter Lombard's *Sentences* developed the idea of a big picture theology and then it became standard to talk about this fourfold state. The writers who used this fourfold state were talking about believers, but Boston was different because he wanted to address the situation of the unsaved and strikingly in his book he leaves hell until the last chapter for that reason. This was intended since his book was worked over several times. He wanted to give a biblical doctrine of hell. His point was that everyone must face death, believers and unbelievers. Two bodies lie in the morgue side by side. There is no way to tell what their eternal destiny is by looking at their outward appearances, but one person has trusted in Christ to save him from their sins and is in heaven and the other is still in his sins and is in hell.

What is hell like?
Boston says,

> God is the chief good and therefore to be separated from him must be the chief evil. Our native country, our relations, and our life are good and therefore to be deprived of them we reckon a great evil; and the better a thing is the greater evil is the loss of it ... The full enjoyment of him (God) is the highest pinnacle of happiness the creature is capable of arriving at: to be fully and finally separated from him must be the lowest step of misery, which the rational creature can be reduced to.[25]

Boston's heart

But Boston wants to be evangelistic. He ends the book by talking about sin and grace and offering Christ. He makes it clear that a decision for or against Christ will have eternal consequences. His last words in the book go like this:

> The terrors of hell, as well as the joys of heaven, are set before you, to stir you up to a cordial receiving of Him, with all His salvation; and to incline you to the way of faith and holiness, in which alone you can escape the everlasting fire. May the Lord Himself make them effectual to that end![26]

This is Boston being evangelistic. He is desperate for sinners to escape hell and instead go to heaven by accepting the *whosoever* promises of the bible. A favourite text of Boston's is Revelation 22:17 where everyone is invited to come and taste the water of life.

> The Spirit and the bride say, 'Come!' And let the one who hears say, 'Come!' Let the one who is thirsty come; and let the one who wishes take the free gift of the water of life.[27]

Boston was involved in what was known as the *Marrow Controversy*, which was an attempt to defend the open offer of the gospel available to all, against the danger of hyper-Calvinism, within Reformed theology. But it is about the subject of hell that Boston is most original. Hell, says Boston, is an awful subject but a necessary one that should be faced up to. He argues that when we water down hell or ignore it we remove one of the gospel's key points. If we are offering Christianity as a better life on earth this is not a strong apologetic since people often find that when they become Christians life gets harder. It's more effective to include hell, argues Boston, because we are explaining why the cross was necessary, and the folly of ignoring its power to save us from judgment. Such biblical realism about the struggle of the Christian life is one of the supreme benefits of studying Puritan writers like Boston.

Boston's concern for the poor

Reformed theology emphasizes what is called *The Cultural Mandate:* the obligation of Christians to live actively in society and work for the transformation of the world and its culture, from Genesis 1:28. There is ample evidence that having heaven in his eye led Boston to also having earth on his heart, expressed by his desire to help others. My wife Gloria and I went to Edinburgh to visit the New College Library to look at some of Boston's original documents. We handled and read his autobiography which was very moving. The library kindly tracked down a letter from Boston to a Mistress Shiell at her lodging in the Castle-hill (Edinburgh) written from Ettrick Manse [November] 25, 1731 and a retired friend from the Records Office in Edinburgh subsequently helped transcribe it for me.

> Dear Mss Shiell
> 'Tis with great pleasure I can tell you now, that our Poor's money, after enduring repeated solicitations in prejudice of it, is wholly recovered, I mean the principal sum of 400 merks.

It is impossible to ascertain the specific circumstances of the letter but it is clear that Boston has had a hand in raising money to help the poor in his parish. Later in the letter, he expresses joy that Christians have been moved to express their faith in deeds of mercy. He writes,

> I wrote to you before, that the liberal thing you devised in favour of John Andison will be very acceptable, be it less or more. Tis the joy of my heart to see people disposed to adorn the doctrine of God's grace with good works, particularly to honour the Lord with their substance. I'm sure the grace of Our Lord Jesus Christ is the most efficacious incentive to it. And I hope 'tis not amiss to tell you, that this poor parish has refreshed my bowels [greatly cheered me] in two instances of it within these few months.

Boston's focus on the priority of heaven gave him a deep concern for people on earth. The oft quoted criticism of such Christians as 'too heavenly minded to be of earthly use', is shown by him to be incorrect. Boston demonstrates that if you are truly heavenly minded you will be of great earthly use!

We now have a raft made up of four planks—*The Fourfold State*; what we need now are some ropes (some Puritan distinctive features) to hold the raft together. Before doing so a brief discussion of the origin and use of the term 'Puritan' would be timely, since it has long had negative connotations suggesting that the Puritans were killjoys!

Who were the Puritans?

I have said that Boston formed a synthesis of what was best about Reformation and Puritan thought but I have not defined the word 'Puritan'. The Oxford English Dictionary has this definition of the noun Puritan:

a member of a group of English Protestants of the late 16th and 17th centuries who regarded the Reformation of the Church under Elizabeth I as incomplete and sought to simplify and regulate forms of worship. A person with censorious moral beliefs, especially about self-indulgence and sex.[28]

The term 'Puritan' was always a smear word from the start in the 1560s but as time has gone on the mud has got thicker! Concern for the purity of God's church was always likely to draw criticism from the world and it has! Whilst the first part of the Oxford Dictionaries definition of 'Puritan' is reasonably accurate about the historical context the second part about *censorious moral beliefs* is loaded with the baggage of previous centuries! These views have been challenged by a series of modern scholars, whose positive insights have been popularized by books like *Worldly Saints: The Puritans As They Really Were* by Leland Ryken and *Among God's Giants: The Puritan Vision of the Christian Life* by J. I. Packer. Packer goes as far as to argue that the Puritans gave us the Christian home.[29] As a result of modern scholarship much of the mud that had accrued to the term 'Puritan' has been washed off and,

informed folk now acknowledge that the typical Puritans were not wild men, fierce and freaky, religious fanatics and social extremists, but sober, conscientious, and cultured citizens: persons of principle, devoted, determined, and disciplined, excelling in domestic virtues, and with no obvious shortcomings except a tendency to run to words when saying anything important, whether to God or man. At least now the record has been set straight.[30]

Different authorities fix the historical parameters of the Puritan era in various ways. Packer says that some see the 'Puritan Century' as 1550–1660 but better to see a Puritan century and a half from 1550–1690s.[31]

This would put Thomas Boston just inside the term 'Puritan' since he was born in 1676.

If the idea of 'heaven in your eye, earth on your heart' is so basic to Puritan thought then we would expect this key feature of their thinking to be strongly linked to their view of heaven. This hypothesis we will now seek to test. I will examine five Puritan features (the ropes of the raft):

• The Bible as normative for life and doctrine;

• Holiness to the Lord;

• The church as the centre of God's plans;

• Bringing order to my disorderly world;

• The church militant.[32]

This last feature I will discuss in relation to the soldier-pilgrims, Richard Baxter, John Bunyan and William Gurnall in Section Two of the book. I will seek to show in this section how each of the five Puritan facets outlined by Puritan expert J. I. Packer is connected to this key thought of heaven in your eye and earth on your heart.

4

Boston's Puritan credentials: The Bible as a guide to heaven and earth

The tiny rafts that my brother Jim and I constructed didn't require much knowledge about sailing and our first venture into the world of dinghy sailing on Windermere was a disaster. Since then I have gained a basic knowledge of sailing that enables me to safely hire dinghies on Ullswater in the Lake District. But now Jim sails a boat for the bank he works for! He has passed all his captains' exams and instructs as well as sails on the ocean. His knowledge of sailing is considerable. In the sailing world new books on the craft of sailing are often promoted under the title of *The Bible of Sailing*. When it comes to the Puritans, the Bible was essential as a rule of life in matters of life and doctrine. The Puritans were a people of the book. They studied it even more carefully than my brother Jim consults his books about sailing! For both sailing and living out the Christian life it is not just about theory but knowledge gained by practice and the application of the truth. Boston was a shepherd-captain who steered his course according to the Bible and conducted his journey towards heaven based upon its light.

The Puritans had a very high view of Scripture and this is our first 'rope' on our imaginary raft. They believed it should be properly interpreted using its context and they saw the importance of the two covenants of law and grace. They believed in the authority of God's word as the rule of life. It was to be applied to every aspect. Today many believers only look at the Covenant of Grace stressing God's love without acknowledging the importance of the Covenant of the Law. Frank Allred describes the common idea

> that God has lowered his standards in the New Covenant. The demand for holiness, it is thought, is not as important under grace as it was under the law. This is a most serious error. The level of obedience God requires is the same in New Testament as it was in the Old. The beneficiaries of the New Covenant are to make every effort to be holy, for 'without holiness, no-one will see the Lord' (Hebrews 12:14).[33]

We will look at holiness for the Puritans in the next chapter.

In the *Fourfold State*, Boston shows his belief in the authority of the Scriptures and the effect of regeneration, he argues, is to make a person trust the Scriptures as God's word:

> The light of grace is an overcoming light, determining men

to assent to divine truths on the mere testimony of God. It is no easy thing for the mind of man to acquiesce in divine revelation.[34]

For Boston, spiritual regeneration that leads to union with Christ is something that he will return to again and again. When a man is born anew into the kingdom of God (John 3:3) he is given a love of the Scriptures. They become normative for his doctrine and life. Following Christ means obeying the Scriptures. Today it is common for people to work from their problem towards the Bible, instead of working out what the Bible says about an ethical issue and then following its teaching no matter how costly that might be.

What does the Bible say about heaven and earth?

The New Testament is constantly exhorting us to live in the light of eternity. It develops themes from the Old Testament and applies them to Jesus. So for example

Jacob dreams of a gateway or stairway to *heaven from the earth* and in John 1:51 Jesus says to Nathanael that he is the gateway to heaven: 'Truly, truly, I say to you, you will see heaven opened, and the angels of God ascending and descending on the Son of Man'.

If you were to ask Jesus to explain in a few sentences what his mission was about he would say it was about a heavenly kingdom and he is the King of that kingdom. Both John the Baptist and Jesus proclaimed: 'Repent, for the Kingdom of heaven is at hand'. We see the importance of heaven in the many parables of the Kingdom: this is a present Kingdom that is growing like mustard seed that becomes a great tree etc. This idea of an epic kingdom is found in modern culture. People identify with popular films like *Gladiator* for example, which is the tale of a felon who dies in order to destroy a wicked Caesar and bring in a new way of thinking about the Roman Empire. Jesus dies a criminal's death and through his death and resurrection defeats the world, the flesh and the devil and brings in an eternal kingdom with himself as its King. When Pontius Pilate asks Jesus if he is a king, he replies that 'My kingdom is not of this world' (John 18:36). Ridley Scott, the director of the film *Gladiator* denies that it is about life after death and yet Maximus, the main character and hero, continuously sees a vision of his murdered wife and son waiting for him in paradise. Addressing his cavalry before outflanking the Gauls, Maximus declares, 'What we do in life echoes in eternity'. John Newton quotes, 'the seeds of eternity are sown in time'. Paul says in Galatians 6:7–8,

> Do not be deceived: God is not mocked, for whatever one sows, that will he also reap. For the one who sows to his own flesh will from the flesh reap corruption, but the one who sows to the Spirit will from the Spirit reap eternal life

Another strong picture in the Bible related to heaven is the idea of renewal. We see this in Boston's raft of the *Fourfold State*. The state of innocence lost through the Fall is partially restored in the state of grace and then fully restored in the state of glory. This expresses the Bible's plot line of Creation, the Fall, Redemption and Renewal. Throughout the Bible, in both Old and New Testaments, miracles point to the fact that the fallen creation will be renewed. Just as Christ is raised from the dead as the first fruits (1 Corinthians 15:20), so the whole creation will be renewed. 2 Peter 3:13 says 'according to his promise we are waiting for new heavens and a new earth in which righteousness dwells'. In Revelation 21, John saw a new heaven and a new earth, for the first heaven and the first earth had passed away.

How does Boston handle the biblical data on heaven and earth?

Boston's focus on heaven is very much on a future reality when Christ comes rather than on a *realized eschatology*, a term that refers to blessings that are for the here and now rather than for the fullness we experience in eternity. Philip Ryken thinks this is probably due to the structure of the *Fourfold State* since the state of grace is not allowed to intrude into the state of glory.[35] However, the impact of keeping heaven in your eye can still have considerable effect on earth. Union with Christ in the state of grace (on earth) inevitably leads to union with Christ in the far higher state of glory in heaven (Romans 8:30). But heaven will not just be a reinstatement of Eden (the state of innocence) that was lost at the Fall but an even higher state. This understanding of the greatness of what is to come in the state of glory is enough to put a spring into the step of every believer, no matter how burdened by the pressures of the world! This is truth to be appropriated now!

Boston is aware of the difficulty of describing heaven, since by definition, it is something beyond our experience and we have to rely on a relatively small amount of biblical data. Why does the Bible talk so little about the details of heaven? It's because the experience of a place is dependent on sharing that experience with another person. We see a wonderful sunset and instinctively we want to share it with a friend. What makes heaven heavenly will be the presence of Jesus. I want to go to heaven because Jesus will be there.

Boston has a positive and negative strategy to overcoming the difficulties of describing heaven says Philip Ryken.[36] Positively, he uses the biblical image of the heavenly kingdom to portray the glories of the eternal state. Negatively, he contrasts the glory of that state with the instability of the state of innocence and the imperfections of the state of grace.

Boston's Preaching Strategy

1. The heavenly kingdom
This image of an epic kingdom is not just seen in popular films like Gladiator but is an idea taken up by C. S. Lewis in the Narnia stories. Aslan the great King makes all the sons of Man into kings and queens under his supremacy.

> In the presence of all their friends and to the sound of trumpets, Aslan solemnly crowned them and led them to the four thrones amid deafening shouts of, 'Long live King Peter! Long live Queen Susan! Long live King Edmund! Long live Queen Lucy!'[37]

This has its basis in Scripture in Revelation 4:4

> Around the throne were twenty-four thrones, and seated on the thrones were twenty-four elders, clothed in white garments, with golden crowns on their heads.

It's most likely, says my former tutor at Oak Hill College Paul Gardner,[38] that the twenty-four elders stand for the patriarchs (the twelve tribes of Israel) and the twelve apostles (representing the New Testament Church). They are dressed in white and have crowns of gold on their heads and sit on thrones suggesting a share in ruling. Crowns have already been mentioned in Revelation as rewards for those who are faithful to Christ in 2:10 and 3:11. This picture in 4:4 represents all God's people who will share in the rule of God and his Christ. Christ will share his kingdom with his people! What an undeserved and remarkable truth to meditate upon. Boston describes it in this way:

> The state of glory is represented under the idea of a kingdom, a kingdom, among men, being that in which the greatest number of earthly good things centre. Now every saint shall, as a king, inherit a kingdom. All Christ's subjects shall be kings, each one with a crown on his head: not that the great King shall divest himself of His royalty, but He will make all His children partakers of His kingdom.[39]

In talking about heaven, Boston realises the need for metaphor and copies the divine accommodation to human limitations:

> As, by familiar resemblances, parents instruct their little children concerning things of which otherwise they can have no tolerable notion; so our gracious God, in consideration of our weakness, is pleased to represent to us heaven's happiness under similitudes taken from earthly things, glorious in the eyes of men.

If God showed us these glories without such condescension they would be too bright for earthly eyes, Boston argues.

2. The glory of the final state (for believers)

Boston uses an approach used by some of his sources to contrast man's eternal state with his present state of grace. This contrast has been used throughout the *Fourfold State*, but now the state of glory shines out far beyond that of the state of grace in powerful ways. Boston does this by outlining features about the state of grace that will not be needed in heaven. There will be no need of public ordinances, no preaching, there will be no need of confession of sin, no self-examination and no Bibles! It will be a country devoid of every frustration of this life and filled with every blessing of the eternal state:

> [Heaven] is a country better than the best of this world; namely the heavenly Canaan, Immanuel's land, where nothing is wanting to complete the happiness of the inhabitants. This is the happy country blessed with a perpetual spring, and yielding all things for necessity, convenience and delight. There man will eat angels' food; they shall be entertained with the hidden manna (Revelation 2:17), without being set to the painful task of gathering it: they will be fed to the full, without the product of the land falling into their mouths, without the least toil to them. That land enjoys everlasting day, for 'there is no night there' (Revelation 21:25). Eternal sunshine beautifies this better country, but there is no scorching heat …[40]

Eternal sunshine and no scorching heat suggest the perfect holiday destination! Think of that holiday in the sun when you wanted to stay forever and never come home. Heaven is like that. My wife and I love to holiday in the Canary Islands during the English Winter with its ideal temperature of 22 degrees centigrade! I swim in the heated pool outside our hired apartment. The climate is the reason we go there. But because of the volcanic ash on the island, it never fails to remind me of the waste heaps outside my Dad's old mine in the North-East! The only plants in the Canary Islands seem to be cacti. In heaven there are perfect temperatures, no ash tips and a beautiful garden city like that at Eden but only better!

Taking up Augustine's thinking Boston reasons that the state of glory is not just a reinstatement of what Adam lost but a higher glory for Mankind:

> How happy might innocent Adam have been in the earthly paradise, where there was nothing wanting for use or delight! Eden was the most pleasant spot of the uncorrupted earth, and paradise the most pleasant spot in Eden: but what is earth compared to heaven? The glorified saints are advanced to the heavenly paradise. There they will not only see but 'eat of the tree of life', which is in the midst of the paradise of God.[41]

Many think that heaven will be what Adam experienced of Eden in his innocence. But Man will be exalted beyond this 'pre-fallen' state. Life will be so much better in heaven than that on Eden's earth! As someone has said, *we gain more than Adam lost.* What a wonderful encouragement to keep going as we battle on earth! This state of glory forms the final log on our raft.

The four logs of the raft

The paradigm used by Boston outlines man's various states as having four 'logs' making up our raft of security for stormy and uncertain days. Understanding this paradigm will give us a Puritan mind and give us the cultivated heart we need to overcome our setbacks and struggles and keep sailing on to heaven.

Log One: The State of Innocence (possible to sin or not to sin).
When God created Adam in the garden he made him in a state of 'innocence', where it was possible for him to sin or not to sin against God. In federal terms this is also called the 'covenant of works'.

Log Two: The State of Sin (not possible not to sin)
Adam by his choice to sin made himself and his descendants 'sinners', not able to resist sin. We are born sinners and we sin (Romans 3:10–12). We are incapable of not sinning, without God's grace to help us. This state rules from Genesis 3 to the second coming of Christ.

Log Three: The State of Grace (possible not to sin)
Whilst we still live under our sinful human natures, alongside that state God gives us new birth into a living hope through the resurrection of Jesus Christ from the dead (1 Peter 1:3). Now we have two natures within us, so we can resist sin or indulge in it. These two natures, new life by the Spirit of God and the old sinful nature are in constant conflict (Galatians 5:17).

Log Four: The State of Glory (not possible to sin)
The arrival of a new heaven and earth will signal the beginning

of this new age of glory. In this state, God has ordained that it will not be possible for man to sin. This state, which was theoretically possible for Adam if he had been obedient during his probation, is on a much higher level than the state of innocence and the state of grace.

This new age will be the fulfilment of the glorious Covenant of Redemption worked out by the Father who sends the Son, the Son who keeps the covenant of works and dies for the elect, and the Holy Spirit who applies the work of salvation to the elect and brings them to heaven. This has been God's great design to have a people for himself. There they will see God:

> This is called the beatific vision, and is the perfection of understanding ... It is but an obscure delineation of the glory of God, that mortals can have on earth; a sight as it were of his back parts (Exodus 33:23) But there they will see his face (Revelation 22:4) ... This blissful sight of God being quite above our present capacities, we must needs be much in the dark about it.[42]

The Image of God in man is fully restored

At Creation Man is made in the image of God (Genesis 1:27); but this image is lost because of the Fall and partly renewed in the state of grace. This image, says Boston, is now completely restored in the state of glory:

> How will the saints be united to God and he to them, when he shall see nothing in them but his own image; when their love will arrive at its perfection, being swallowed up in their glorious transformation into the likeness of God.[43]

We shall share God's likeness and fulfil his perfect will for our lives. *The Westminster Confession of Faith* defined the chief end of man as being *to glorify God and enjoy him forever.* Heaven is not just a great place to spend eternity; it's the place where God and Jesus the Lamb of God live.

Revelation 21:3 says, 'They will be his people, and God himself will be with them as their God'

At the end of the Bible there are wonderful images of streets of gold, an emotional homecoming for God's people and the absence of suffering sorrow or death. What a glorious future to look forward to in heaven.

Charles Stanley uses the same approach as Boston by comparing heaven to something very familiar on earth, a happy home:

> Think about the comfortable feeling you have as you open your front door. That's but a hint of what we'll feel some day on arriving at the place our Father has lovingly and personally prepared for us in heaven. We will finally—and permanently— be 'at home' in a way that defies description.[44]

5

Boston's Puritan credentials:
Holiness to the Lord

In this chapter we turn to the second 'rope' around our imaginary raft of security, holiness to the Lord. Biblical holiness is being set apart for the Lord. Barclay in his commentary on Hebrews says,

> Although he lives in the world, the man who is hagios (Greek for holy) must always in one sense be different from the world and separate from the world. His standards are not the world's standards.[45]

However, worldliness has often been a major feature within the church through its history. My brother Jim and I sometimes got our feet wet in our amateur rafts, because the ropes were not tight enough or strong enough and the planks parted and water came in. Or we decided to dangle our feet over the side of the raft. If the raft represents the biblical worldview, we often get our feet wet in the church when we step outside the Bible's teaching and dangle our feet in the world. Bishop J. C. Ryle, another fan of the Puritans, wisely said: 'Open transgression of God's Law slays its thousands, but worldliness slays its tens of thousands'.[46]

Holiness to the Lord was a great slogan of the Puritans, who recognised the need to challenge worldliness in the church and nation. They held to a pietistic outlook that sees personal holiness and holiness of community as of crucial importance. They wanted the glory of God in church and state; in other words they wanted to make their church and state pleasing to God. To accomplish this they became pastors and evangelists in order to convert England. They campaigned vigorously in every area of life: religious, political and social to make England a land pleasing to the Lord. Again the perspective of eternity played a big part. They would echo the Lord's Prayer, *Hallowed be your name ... on earth as it is in heaven.*

Boston's Scotland

Christianity was at a low level in the Scotland of his day. In his autobiography he writes about his prayer regarding whether to answer a call to the church at Simprin.[47] He describes his struggle in coming to a decision to accept the call as due to: *1. The rarity of the godly there and in the country; 2. The very smallness of their number.*— 'His handful' as he often termed his flock. Yet by the time he came to move on to his next charge there had been considerable spiritual growth. His book the *Fourfold State*, which was the fruit of his preaching at Simprin had a massive impact in improving the spiritual state of Scotland for many years after his death. His influence for good was felt on all levels of society since even ordinary folk were able to read his book. In the Dutch Reformed church his book is still held in high regard. I think we should see a revival of interest in his theology across the church once more to restore this raft of security which helped so many in a time of religious and social confusion like ours. It is part of the purpose of this book to alert more Christians to the blessings of reading Puritans like Thomas Boston. He is a great shepherd-captain. Study of his writings will give us spiritual refreshment for the journey to heaven and help restore biblical holiness to the church.

Something has gone deeply wrong in the Western church

In much of our contemporary Christian culture being happy has eclipsed the desire to be holy. As I believe Packer once said, 'Most of us live (almost) like Marxists' in practical terms, only living for this world without much thought or care about the world that is to come. Sadly, this mindset has led to a great deal of worldliness in the church, including those who call themselves conservative evangelicals. Sometimes this manifests itself in ungodly manipulation by a minister of a congregation and sometimes by harsh treatment of ministers by congregations. My wife and I have experienced it from both sides of the fence! These were the circumstances I was referring to right at the beginning of the book which caused such deep hurt to me and my family. We managed by the grace of God and the support of godly friends to come through these experiences but there are many who have left the church altogether because of such ingrained and sinful behaviour patterns. I acknowledge with John Newton that *I am a great sinner and Christ is a great Saviour* and that I am not innocent of fault in these failures. However there is something deeply wrong in many churches where there is a lack of spiritual resources for practical repentance with many folk unprepared to admit personal responsibility, make amends and strive for reconciliation. We deeply lack biblical holiness. Dallas Willard has this sobering criticism of the conservative side of the church

> A fundamental mistake of the conservative side of the church today is that it takes its basic goal to get as many people as possible ready to die and go to heaven. It aims to get people into heaven rather than to get heaven into people. This of course requires that people who are going to be in heaven must be right on what is basic. You can't really quarrel with that. But it turns out that to be right on 'what is basic' is to be right in terms of the particular church tradition in question, not in terms of Christlikeness.[48]

At face value, Dallas Willard seems to contradict the thesis of this book that if we aim at heaven we get earth thrown in! However, what Dallas Willard seems to be getting at is a view of Christianity that is superficial and not based on 'what is basic' (authentic Biblical belief and practice) but on a particular church tradition that has no impact on earth in terms of Christlikeness and turns out to be unloving to its own members and those outside. Willard ascribes this 'fundamental mistake' to the *conservative side of the church* as a whole, as if holding a conservative view leads to such an antithesis of 'genuine spiritual transformation or full-throttle discipleship of Jesus Christ'.[49] Thomas Boston and the Puritans refute this since they had a 'doctrine for life' that clearly led to Christlikeness. Perhaps most of us know loving churches that hold 'theologically conservative views' that would also contradict Willard's statement? I certainly do!

Willard is right to say that getting heaven into people should be the aim rather than simply getting people into heaven. Both I would argue are very important. The value of Willard's provocative statement is to make us look more deeply into the impact of having heaven in our eye on our lives on earth and I will come back to this challenge throughout the book. It is undeniable that there have been catastrophic failures in some churches that call themselves conservative, as there have been in all sorts of churches. In a section entitled *Something is rotten in the church*, Willard lays bare the catalogue of failures amongst prominent Christian leaders that

> might make us think genuine spiritual formation in Christlikeness to be impossible for real human beings ... And the failures that become known are few compared to the ones that remain relatively unknown and even accepted among Christians.[50]

Willard is speaking about the church in America but the church across the Atlantic in the U.K. shows similar features to that in the United States. He goes on to describe the cover-up and acceptance of open sin amongst pastors and congregations. As well as these disturbing features of the modern church he recounts a general worldliness of congregations where failures in the area of sex and money are joined by 'the presence of vanity, egoism, hostility, fear, indifference and downright meanness ... amongst professing Christians'.[51]

Willard is right to see the 'central cause of our current situation … is simple distraction'.[52] He quotes Leith Anderson in his very helpful assessment of contemporary church life who notes:

> While the New Testament speaks often about churches, it is surprisingly silent about many matters that we associate with church structure and life. There is no mention of architecture, pulpits, lengths of typical sermons, rules for having Sunday school. Little is said about styles of music, order of worship, or times of church gatherings. There were no Bibles, denominations, camps, pastors' conferences, or board meeting minutes. Those who strive to be New Testament churches must seek to live its principles and absolutes, not produce the details.[53]

The Puritans can help!
Whilst the Puritans had their faults they produced an authentic expression of New Testament Christianity based on its *principles and absolutes*. Whilst they lived in a culture very different from ours they lived in times of uncertainty like today and they can offer us a heavenly-minded theology that led to Christlikeness on earth. Their watchword was 'holiness to the Lord' and the rediscovery of biblical holiness is what is needed in today's church to address the issues raised by Dallas Willard above.

I would like to offer two insights from Thomas Boston and one from the more recent East African Revival which took place in the 1930s and 1970s beginning in Rwanda and spreading to Kenya and Uganda. My wife Gloria was a missionary with Rwanda Mission in the 1980s and saw the effects of the revival.

I have just returned from Nairobi where I have been part of the second Global Anglican Future Conference (GAFCON) attended by 1400 delegates from 38 countries. One of the reasons East Africa was chosen was because of the revival there. The first day of the conference was devoted to hearing speakers touched by the revival in the 1970s and many are now senior pastors and evangelists. One of the seminars showing concern for the state of the Western church was entitled: *Gospel and Culture: How can we re-evangelize the West?* Given the deeply seated problems already outlined in the Western church what can be done to restore holiness?

First we need to see the importance of being in union with Christ; second we need the empowering of the Holy Spirit to bring radical repentance and third we need to restore the importance of the conscience informed by Scripture in order for this change to be lasting.

1. Union with Christ

Boston puts regeneration before union with Christ. He uses it here to describe the essential nature of the new birth. This must precede union with Christ since we are initially united with Christ in regeneration (Ephesians 2:4–5). Spiritual regeneration that leads to union with Christ is central for Boston. Without holiness we cannot enter heaven and without regeneration we cannot be holy, because our holiness is imputed through union with Christ.

> Regeneration is absolutely necessary to qualify you for heaven. None go there but those who are made meet for it (Colossians 1:12).[54]

Regeneration is absolutely necessary to your being admitted to heaven (John 3:3). No heaven without it … There is no holiness without regeneration. 'It is the new man which is created in true holiness' (Ephesians 4:24). And no heaven without holiness; 'for without holiness no man shall see the Lord' (Hebrews 12:14).[55]

But Boston also uses regeneration in a second way to describe the regenerate life (i.e. sanctification) that follows the new birth. Boston outlines the radical change towards holiness that regeneration brings to the redeemed sinner, who has new appetites:

He desires to be holy as well as happy; and rather to be gracious than great. His hopes, which before were low, and fastened down to things on earth—are now raised, and set on the glory which is to be revealed. He entertains the hope of eternal life, grounded on the word of promise, Titus 1:2.[56]

Boston bases his quest for holiness in his hope of heaven made possible through union with Christ.

Boston's call to spiritual regeneration that leads to union with Christ expressed in biblical holiness needs to be understood as essential once more. W. E. Sangster, the Methodist preacher, echoes Boston's New Testament approach. When I first became a Christian, whilst at teacher-training college in Liverpool, a Christian couple took me 'under their wing' and helped disciple me. They gave me a copy of *Daily Readings by* W. E. Sangster.[57] In the opening page they wrote 'Page 272' and the date: 'September 1974'. When I turned to the page it was entitled *This Life is Possible to All.* I have never forgotten it. In those pages Sangster issues a challenge to holiness:

> Rare as saints now are, they could (in the New Testament sense) be common. Nothing but our faithlessness and indiscipline prevents us from joining this high company.

This was clearly one of Sangster's deep concerns for in another piece *Why the Church Needs Saints*, he writes,

> It cannot seriously be questioned that it is a matter of major importance that the admiration of people be directed towards those who are worthy of the admiration. We grow like the people we admire. If the longing for holiness is to be quickened in people they must see, not only its perfection in the Saviour, but approximations to it in the saints. Indeed, there are ways in which it could be perilous to see it only in the Saviour and never in the saints.[58]

Sangster then outlines four steps to quicken the quest for holiness in people-

> First, to convince people that it is God's intention that man should be holy; Secondly, to nourish in the people faith in the possibility of holiness; Thirdly, to hold perfection before the people in all its fullness in Jesus. By a strange contortion of the human mind the very perfection of Our Lord's example is used to excuse men from following it. Fourthly to see disclosed the great ministry of the saints. Their holiness is all derived. It is begotten in them of God—begotten in that very human

nature which man in self-despair had recognized as hopeless and corrupt.[59]

Sangster has his own answer to the weakness of the church:

> Nothing but an increase of saints will make the church powerful in the world. The Holy Spirit is the Lord and Giver of Life. As He comes to sanctify, so He comes in power. The world could not long ignore a holy church. The church is not despised because it is holy: it is despised because it is not holy enough.

Willard's critique of the church mentioned earlier is devastating. He poses the question, 'What is to be done?' and says, 'a reasonable response might be that these local congregations would be entirely devoted to the spiritual formation of those in attendance to the "renovation of the heart", as we have called it here'.[60]

He is surely right that there is a serious lack of godliness in the contemporary church and a great deal of worldliness. How can this 'spiritual formation' to help remedy the situation be achieved? Boston and Sangster have taught us the first thing we need: the vital teaching of union with Christ. Boston tells us that 'Regeneration is absolutely necessary to qualify you for heaven' and Sangster tells us that 'their holiness is all derived … Nothing but our faithlessness and indiscipline prevents us from joining this high company' [of believers experiencing 'approximations' of the holiness of Christ in their daily lives]. All our holiness comes from union with Christ and this makes us fit for heaven and for service on earth.

2. Prayer for a move of the Holy Spirit
to bring radical repentance

Sangster also points to the second feature that is required in restoring holiness to our local churches when he says 'The Holy Spirit is the Lord and Giver of Life. As He comes to sanctify, so He comes in power'. To this vital need we now turn for insights gained from the East African Revival, which resulted in public repentance and 'walking in the light', and whose impact is still felt deeply today.

God's church has been sustained by such revivals. In 2 Chronicles we see six revivals which all begin by the people of God seeking the Lord. God the Father answers and sends his Holy Spirit in power. We are so deeply rooted in individualism and materialism in the Western church that we need a mighty revival from God like that seen in East Africa. It started as all revivals do with a small group of concerned believers gathering regularly and crying out to God in sustained prayer. Joe Church was one of those whose heart longed for 'reality' with God. As they sought the Lord together, God the Holy Spirit brought a wonderful revival to East Africa. Wisely the leaders of the revival were able to keep it within the existing church structures preserving unity of the Spirit. Their effective vision was to establish schools, hospitals and churches at strategic locations. There was, as Joe wrote, 'a spirit of adventure for God, given by the Holy Spirit, that caused us to claim in faith four new sites for mission stations covering the whole of Ruanda-Urindi'.[61]

At the conference I attended in Nairobi I was moved by the stories of lives turned from worldliness to godliness by the power of God during that revival, which was still producing holy people thirty years after the second outpouring happened. God is sovereign and we cannot order or demand a revival but in 2 Chronicles 7:14 it gives a generic statement of what to do if your nation needs one and Britain certainly needs this urgently.

> if my people who are called by my name humble themselves, and pray and seek my face and turn from their wicked ways, then I will hear from heaven and will forgive their sin and heal their land.

3. The restoration of the conscience informed by Scripture

If this focus on regeneration leading to ongoing and daily repentance and change of life is to be sustained it must go deep and affect the whole person. Joe Church and the other leaders of the East African revival maintained that the teaching of the Bible must be kept central if the revival was not to lose its momentum. One of the major expressions of the revival was the focus on public repentance as consciences were touched by the Holy Spirit. Apparently upright Christians confessed to stealing funds and made restitution. Immoral behaviour and unloving acts were repented of and amends made to bring closure. Boston, with the rest of the Puritans, also believed in the critical importance of the use of conscience once it is renewed by the Spirit of God and informed by the word of God. He likens the renewal of the conscience to a candle being *snuffed and brightened,* to expose darkness in the recesses of the heart, so that hidden faults and sins can seen and be healed. He describes the awakened conscience as follows:

> As a new light is set up in the soul, in regeneration,

conscience is enlightened, instructed and informed. That candle of the Lord, Proverbs 20:27, is now snuffed and brightened; so that it shines, and sends forth its light into the most retired corners of the heart: discovering sins which the Conscience, which lay sleeping in the man's bosom before, is now awakened, and makes its voice to be heard through the whole soul; therefore, there is no more rest for him in the sluggard's bed; he must get up and be doing, arise, 'haste, and escape for his life.'[62]

Puritanism sees the conscience as being the key to sanctification. The desire for a clean conscience is motivated by our progress towards heaven, where there will be no sin. In the *The State of Glory,* Boston, following Augustine, says that the children of God will not be able to sin. In our present *State of Grace,* it is possible not to sin. However we still retain our old sinful natures carried over from the *State of Sin,* as we wait for the return of Christ. We therefore have a choice, as Adam did in the *The State of Innocence* where it is possible to sin or not to sin. However, unlike us Adam did not have a sinful nature until he chose to take the forbidden fruit from the tree and mankind entered the *The State of Sin* making it impossible not to sin. This is why regeneration leading to union with Christ is so vital, because through Christ we enter a state of grace which will certainly end in the state of glory (see Romans 8:30). Our progress towards holiness in this life ready for the next becomes a major preoccupation. In the struggle against our old sinful nature, that wars against the new nature (Galatians 5:17) the biblical understanding and use of conscience is crucial.

All the Reformers saw the use of conscience as critical to a reformed faith. Luther regarded the question of conscience as vital. At the Diet of Worms, he was asked to recant and admit publicly that his books and the ideas contained in them were wrong. He asked for a day and a night to think about his answer, since he was very aware of what could happen to him. Finally after wrestling in prayer all night, he declared that,

> his conscience was captive to the will of God and to go against conscience was neither right nor safe ... Here I stand I can do no other. God help me.

To show the importance of keeping a clear conscience before God let me illustrate this from my own experience in the Church of England. In another Diocese from where I am now, I was told by the area bishop that he was in favour of practicing homosexuals being ordained in the Church of England. He also said that his view was based upon the Bible! I replied that he could not be reading the same Bible as me, since in my Bible homosexual practice was clearly sinful! Since we were about to have this bishop take our confirmation service, I felt I had to report our conversation to my church council, who were shocked that a bishop would make such comments. The upshot was that we refused to have this bishop, until he acknowledged publicly the orthodox and biblical position on human sexuality held to by the Anglican Communion when it met at Lambeth in 1998 (known as Lambeth 1:10). All four bishops from the Diocese closed ranks and refused to come. The main Diocesan bishop spent three separate meetings with me in order to change my mind, which lasted a total of five hours! I repeatedly said in answer to his demands that we back down, 'Bishop, I would like to help you out, but it's my conscience. One day I will stand before God in eternity. Whilst I accept your authority as my bishop, I must bow before a greater authority when the plain truth of Scripture is being undermined'. I'm happy to say that it all ended well with the Diocesan bishop bravely signing Lambeth 1:10, enabling him to lead us in our confirmation service and bringing our public dispute to an end.

Thomas Boston outlines the power of a good conscience, submitted to the word of God, when he writes,

> It powerfully incites to obedience, even in the most spiritual acts, which lie not within the view of the natural conscience; and powerfully restrains from sin, even from those sins which do not lie open to the observation of the world. It urges the sovereign authority of God, to which the heart is now reconciled, and which it willingly acknowledges. And so it engages the man to his duty, whatever be the hazard from the world; for it fills the heart so with the fear of God—that the force of the fear of man is broken.[63]

The fear of God is related to meeting God in glory. The power of a good conscience has been borne out in my experience. I was faced with disciplinary action and possible dismissal by the bishop but I feared God more than the bishop. We can, of course, suppress our conscience. When that temptation comes I find that my conscience speaks up, when I would prefer it to remain silent. When conscience speaks, it stands over us, as if it is distinct from us. We didn't give it this authority, God did. It is as the Puritans called it, *God's watchman of the soul*. This fits with what the Bible says about conscience and our actual experience confirms this. The conscience is a sounding board for God's word to be applied to our lives. A good conscience points us to Christ and to the way of holiness. Thomas Boston concludes

> This has engaged many to put their life in their hand, and follow the cause of Christ, which they once despised, and resolutely walk in the path they formerly abhorred, Galatians 1:23, 'He who persecuted us in times past, now preaches the faith which once he destroyed'.[64]

Holiness to the Lord needs to be restored as a major priority in the modern church. It is striking that three of the four Puritans I have chosen to study faced time in prison or had a close relative who did so. In their concern for holiness of life, they were prepared to suffer for it, rather than compromise their convictions and harm their consciences. They were able to do this because they were so conscious of eternity. How many of us would be prepared to follow their godly example today? A time of persecution may be coming upon the church in the U.K. I believe that within five years we may see vicars and other ministers given prison sentences for opposition to the gay agenda. The egalitarian bandwagon, will not allow exemption for matters of conscience since to reject this is seen by many as a refusal to accept responsibilities as citizens of a pluralistic nation. In the last six months we have seen the arrest of several street preachers who have been released without charge after preaching against sexual sin in the public square. This is just the beginning.

Underneath this demand for equality is a rejection of legitimate difference and a soft Marxism that denies the right to private judgment that has been part of our national laws for centuries. Whilst condemning all homophobic attitudes and repenting of any expression of such sinful attitudes in the church we must resist the pressure of the world's culture to squeeze us into its mould, by graciously insisting on the clear teaching of the Bible that sexual intercourse outside of monogamous marriage of one man and one woman, whether heterosexual or homosexual, is contrary to the will of God and therefore sinful. The example of the Puritans will become more important as time goes on as this oppressive juggernaut denying the teaching of the Bible gathers pace. It was said at the conference at Nairobi by one of the English delegation that *there has never been a reformation in England without blood on the streets.* We, like the Puritans, must 'wage the good warfare, holding faith and a good conscience' (1 Timothy 1:18–19). In the church we must think more about holiness rather than happiness since, we should 'Strive ... for the holiness without which no one will see the Lord' (Hebrews 12:14).

6

Boston's Puritan credentials: The Church is at the centre of God's plans

Spiritual Revival

When my brother Jim and I built and floated a raft, we always invited other children to join us. It was a raft to share. John Donne famously said, 'No man is an island'. The Puritans were not individualists but were united in their concern to win the nation for Christ. This desire arose from their concern to have heaven in their eye and earth on their heart. They were Churchmen whose main concern was that the Church in England existed for the glory of God, since it was God's church. As we saw in the last chapter, this concern for the glory of the Lord led to a passion for holiness. The Puritans were faithful churchmen but when the establishment of the visible church would not accept change they became reforming churchmen. The Puritans lost every battle they fought in terms of reforming the Church of England and the political structures. They did have more success in spreading the gospel to the nation. Thomas Boston was, of course, a Scottish Presbyterian but he still wanted to reform the church and was an excellent shepherd-captain who saw the church at the centre of God's plans to have a people for his own possession. Boston's passion for heaven energized his striving for a renewed church that would be holy to the Lord and win souls to Christ.

Since its inception in 1992, the campaigning group Reform, within the Church of England, has had the overarching aim of reaching the nation for Christ and seeking to, *rock the boat in order to rock it back into position*, in the words of its first chairman, Philip Hacking. I was involved in Reform from the start and have been an enthusiastic supporter ever since, taking part in many of its conferences and occasionally speaking at them. In 2011 I was invited to speak to the Reform National Conference about ministry in urban settings, drawing on my experience in four urban parishes over twenty-five years of ministry. Reform has the same aims as the Puritans of constant reformation, believing that the Church of England needs to be reformed by the application of the Scriptures to be a more faithful church. J. I. Packer observes that 'spiritual revival was central to what the Puritans professed to be seeking. Remarkably, this fact is rarely highlighted and often ignored'.[65] The Puritan ideal of keeping heaven in their eye led to this deep concern for spiritual renewal on earth that would lead to a holy church and nation.

In England the Fellowship of Independent Evangelical Churches (FIEC) has experienced significant growth in recent years as it has sought to be true to the Scriptures and reach out with the gospel. They have grown to a partnership of over five hundred churches supported by a national staff of twelve. On their website it says: 'Sharing the good news of Jesus Christ must be the very heartbeat of all FIEC churches. As we grasp the wonder of his character, the work of the cross and the lostness of the lost, then we must be passionate about proclaiming and demonstrating the truth of the gospel. It must become part of our DNA'. This missionary vision is underpinned by a sound view of heaven and hell: 'The Lord Jesus Christ will return in glory. He will raise the dead and judge the world in righteousness. The wicked will be sent to eternal punishment and the righteous will be welcomed into a life of eternal joy in fellowship with God. God will make all things new and will be glorified forever'. The Puritans would be very happy with both the FIEC passion for mission and their view of the future.

Reaching the nation through a revived church

The Puritans believed that the Church is at the centre of God's purposes and this is the third 'rope' on our imaginary raft. Whilst the gospel calls upon each person to respond individually and teaches that no one can do it for you, becoming a believer does not turn you into a Christian *lone ranger*. We are made for fellowship and the Puritans recognised this. God's plan is stated throughout Scripture as regards the elect: *I will be your God and you will be my people*. God initiates a covenant relationship with his people who are called to faith and obedience (Exodus 6:7, Jeremiah 30:22 and John 10:14–16). To the first two promises are added a third: 'I will write it on their hearts' (Jeremiah 31:33). The Apostle Peter expresses this covenant call as, 'To those who are elect exiles of the Dispersion ... according to the foreknowledge of God the Father, in the sanctification of the Spirit, for obedience to Jesus Christ and for sprinkling with his blood' (1 Peter 1:1–2).

The Puritans believed that the true church is the invisible gathering of the redeemed with Christ as its head, seen in passages such as Hebrews 12:22–23 'But you have come to Mount Zion and to the city of the living God, the heavenly Jerusalem, and to innumerable angels in festal gathering, and to the assembly of the firstborn who are enrolled in heaven'. *The church is not an institution or building but a spiritual reality. This is why the Puritans called their church buildings 'meeting houses'.*[66]

Again the FIEC website has a fine definition of the Church:

> The universal Church is the body of which Christ is the head and to which all who are saved belong. It is made visible in local churches, which are congregations of believers who are committed to each other for the worship of God, the preaching of the Word, the administering of Baptism and the Lord's Supper; for pastoral care and discipline, and for evangelism. The unity of the body of Christ is expressed within and between churches by mutual love, care and encouragement. True fellowship between churches exists only where they are faithful to the gospel.[67]

Fellowship with God in Christ leads to a strong desire for holiness in his church. When they saw their beloved Church of England in such a terrible mess, it would have been irresponsible for the Puritans simply to have ignored what was going on and just got on with parish ministry while they waited for heaven. Their clarion call which we need today was *obeying God rather than men* (Acts 4:19), and they recognized that heeding God's call will sometimes involve entering into controversy and taking action. Packer says that the Puritans were *great fighters and therefore great sufferers.* They never forgot they belonged to a family whom they were responsible to lead and feed with God's word. Their strategy was to reach the nation for Christ by becoming pastors and evangelists across the land. As we will see in Chapter Eight they were prepared to fight for the gospel and so should we today.

Boston as pastor and evangelist

Thomas Boston shared this concern for the wider church in his work as a *great divine*, as Jonathan Edwards called him, but he was also devoted to his work as a pastor and evangelist in Scotland. He rode on horseback across more than one hundred square miles of his parish to visit each family in his church twice a year for spiritual conference or to instruct in the catechism. Whilst he suffered from depression and physical weakness he was never absent from his pulpit in more than thirty years of pastoral ministry. When he was dying, in true Puritan fashion members of his congregation waited outside the window of his manse to hear some special word from their pastor before Christ took him finally to the celestial city. This perseverance and dedication to his calling is inspiring and encouraging. He is a great shepherd-captain. He truly exemplifies the Puritan ideal of the loving shepherd of the sheep, perfectly expressed in John chapter 10:11 by the Lord Jesus himself in his ministry when he declares, 'I am the good shepherd. The good shepherd lays down his life for the sheep'.

In the state of grace, Boston writes about the effect

of regeneration changing the company of the new believer
in Christ. Once again we see the central importance of
regeneration and union with Christ in Boston's theology.

> Formerly, he despised the company of the saints—but now
> they are 'the excellent, in whom is all his delight,' Psalm 16:3.
> 'I am a companion of all who fear you,' says the royal psalmist,
> Psalm 119:63. A renewed man joins himself with the saints; for
> he and they are like-minded, in that which is their main work
> and business; they have all one new nature: they are all travelling
> to Immanuel's land, and converse together in the language of
> Canaan.[68]

What a wonderful picture of the true Church, a band of
brothers headed for Immanuel's land with heaven in their
eye and earth on their heart! This picture contradicts Dallas
Willard's contention that the conservative side of the church
today, discussed in chapter five, is flawed because of its 'basic
goal to get as many people as possible ready to die and go
to heaven. It aims to get people into heaven rather than to
get heaven into people'. Boston shows that a renewed man
joins himself with the saints in loving fellowship travelling
to Immanuel's land. We saw in chapter five how Boston sees
regeneration as essential: both as the means to a new birth
and a subsequent growth in holiness or to use Willard's term,
Christlikeness. As we aim at heaven we get earth thrown in as
our renewed lives are transformed.

Boston shows that all true Christians are brothers and sisters
travelling to the heavenly country together. The Puritans give
us encouragement to work together in gospel partnerships.

Thomas Boston and the Puritans did have their differences. Some were Presbyterians like Boston, some Baptists like Bunyan and some Episcopalians like Baxter, but they agreed with each other on all the basic issues. This was because they believed they had achieved purity of doctrine by developing the Westminster Confession and Catechisms. They held different views on secondary matters but were essentially a single school of thought. Today it is still possible to partner with other gospel-minded folk although evangelicalism is a much broader constituency. When running town-wide missions I have often partnered with FIEC and other churches under the Evangelical Alliance definition of faith. Having established a sound basis of faith in the organising committee you can then throw an invitation out to everyone, church and non-church, to attend.

Heaven in your eye *and* earth on your heart

Boston shows how eternity and the power of grace brings a single-minded concern for gospel work and the spiritual good of others in the world,

> they espouse the interests of religion, and 'prefer Jerusalem above their chief joy,' Psalm 137:6. However privately they live, grace gives them a public spirit, will concern itself in the ark and work of God, in the Gospel of God, and in the people of God, even in those of them whom they never saw. As children of God, they naturally care for these things. They have a new concern for the spiritual good of others: no sooner do they taste of the power of grace themselves—but they are inclined to set up to be agents for Christ and holiness in the world.[69]

This quotation shows that Boston had heaven in his eye and

earth on his heart. He talks of believers who prefer 'Jerusalem', but share together a concern for the spiritual good of others who don't belong to Christ. With a Puritan spirit he lived with the tension of rejecting but also embracing the world for Christ's sake. It also demonstrates that for the Puritans being public spirited, and having a deep concern for *the ark and work of God*, went hand in hand. *Holiness to the Lord* was the Puritans chief concern and the promotion of this helped them to seek a reformed church and nation.

Love to the brethren Boston says will be a strong feature of their churches, because God's love is in them: 'Happy they are who love them merely for grace in them; for their heaven-born temper and disposition; who can pick this pearl even out of infirmities in and about them; lay hold of it, and love them for it'.[70] Such Christian people shine as lights in a dark world and attract others to the Lord Jesus who is the source of their character.

Packer says that the Puritans were *reformed mediaevalists*, so church and state form one community in their thinking. As concepts church and state are distinct, but they thought that those who belonged to one belonged to the other. They were a nation under God, where state and church were one. It was their goal for both church and state, to be *holy to the Lord* their great watchword and slogan.

In our modern world, church and state are two distinct entities except in England, where the Church of England remains the state church. Since the General Synod vote in November 2012 that failed to pass the women bishop legislation because those opposed were not given adequate provision, there have been renewed calls for disestablishment of church and state. This would produce a constitutional crisis since, *no bishops, no King*. This statement is attributed to James the VI of Scotland and I of England, who inherited an emerging reformed church, the Kirk that wanted to get rid of parishes, Diocese and bishops. However on becoming King of England James saw the bishops as natural allies because he believed that the Apostolic Succession of bishops strengthened and supported the divine right of Kings. At the Hampton Court Conference in 1604 the Puritans were pressing for episcopacy to be reformed but James declared his support for the bishops using the phrase, 'no bishops, no King'. Melvyn Bragg in *The Book of Books* about the impact of the *King James Bible* says the Puritans had a point. He goes on to say that the publication of the King James Bible was empowering to democracy in sowing seeds of liberation by putting the Bible into ordinary people's hands in the vernacular. He also has a chapter seeking to demolish Richard Dawkins who wants all trace of religion removed from the public square.

> God and the Bible are once again in the stocks. In the process, many of the achievements which owe their origins to the King James Bible have been diminished, or bypassed or denied. There is now a very fashionable version, some might say a distortion of its history and its impact, which flows from the current ideology of atheism. In the furious effort to raze religion from the surface of the earth much else—that is to say much that religion generates which is not itself primarily religious—is being unjustly downgraded or ignored.[71]

Clearly folk like Richard Dawkins are no friends of church

establishment, but is it time for the church and state to be
finally separated and bishops removed from the House of Lords?

Argument in favour and against disestablishment seems
finely balanced. The Church of England is not meant to be
the chaplain to the nation but an instrument of the mission
of God and disestablishment may help it to get back to that
task. Others argue that we would lose a voice in the heart
of government if the church was disestablished. However,
the government's determination to force through same-sex
marriage, which was not in any of the main political parties'
manifestos and following a flawed consultation process, when
a petition of over 600,000 signatures was effectively ignored,
suggests there is little if any desire to accommodate the core
values of the Church in the seat of power even when such
a large number express their views. Of course one example
of the relationship not working doesn't make the case for
disestablishment and it is difficult to calculate lost influence on
promoting the values of the Church if it went ahead. Perhaps
it's rather like the argument for evangelicals seeking to become
bishops? It's a good thing provided they remain true to the
Scriptures. In the same way those who have influence in the
public square and believe the gospel need to stand up and use
their influence rather than remain silent.

Groups like the Christian Institute and Christian Concern
have helped galvanize opposition to the redefinition of
marriage, the greatest social change in many years, and are
helping the church speak with one voice in the public square.
The Puritans took the same approach of engagement with the
society of the day out of their concern for the purity of the

Church and its active involvement in the world as salt and light, whilst keeping its eye on the world to come. Both evangelism and social action should be going on in the local church right across the nation.

What about bishops?

Bishops promise at their consecration to drive away false teaching, but sometimes they fail to do so. This weakens the witness and unity of the church. In such situations it falls to local vicars to fulfil the promise they made at their ordinations to defend the gospel. In the Prayer Book 'Ordering of Priests', the Bishop says: 'Will you be ready with all faithful diligence, to banish and drive away all erroneous and strange doctrines contrary to God's word; and to use both publick and private monitions and exhortations?' At my ordination in Chester Cathedral in 1989, I was asked that question and I responded by saying solemnly, 'I will, the Lord being my helper'. I have always sought to do this with grace as well as truth. My slogan in the parish and in the diocese is: 'Be loving and firm'. That has involved exercising discipline, as the Ordering of Priests puts it, 'by both public and private means', in order to drive away false doctrine or deal with moral failure. On occasions following the pattern of Matthew 18:15–17, I have withdrawn Holy Communion from church members living in sin. This has always been used as a last resort and has been done with a desire to restore the fallen after repentance and strengthen God's flock (1 Corinthians 5:13). Sometimes I have had to gently remind some bishops of their consecration vows to uphold sound doctrine and drive away error. I teach the folk in my local church not only to make assessments of the soundness of preachers by what they affirm but also by what they fail to say, what Luther called *sinful silence*. Faithful gospel preaching, like Boston in the *Fourfold State*, warns of hell and the wrath to come combined with an open invitation to receive the gospel message of forgiveness and new life with the promise of heaven and fellowship with God forever.

The central importance of mission to the church

In his classic work, *Transforming Mission*, David Bosch wrote, 'mission is not primarily an activity of the church, but an attribute of God. God is a missionary God'.[72] Since God is mission-hearted so should be the church! Mission ought to be at the heart of everything from the welcome a person gets at the church door, to the quality of the preaching and the music to the tea and biscuits afterwards! Making sure the loos are properly cleaned and supplied is also part of what I mean by being concerned about the totality of mission. From the moment a new person enters the church building every part of what they experience is to be missional. Mission must be our heartbeat as it is God's. He is a God of mission to his lost world. Taking the gospel out from our church buildings into our work, our families and into the public square is as important today as it was in Puritan times.

During my twenty-five years of ministry in the Church of England I have had many positive opportunities to work collaboratively with other congregations of evangelical conviction across the denominations in missions. In 1998 I was privileged to chair the Luis Palau Mission to Barnsley, involving over a hundred congregations in Barnsley and the surrounding area. We hired the local Metrodome Leisure Centre for a series of meetings open to the public for a ten day mission. The local police had declined to offer any extra help with traffic control since they judged that, 'few folk in Barnsley would be interested in a Christian mission'. On the first night of the mission, I am pleased to say, that the traffic was stopped in the centre of Barnsley by the large number of people making their way to hear the gospel. There were many who made professions of faith during that exciting mission where the wider Church in Barnsley, aided by a gifted evangelist and his team, were used to bring many folk to Christ and confound, to God's glory, the negative views of the local constabulary. Boston and his fellow Puritans would have been thrilled because they saw the church as being central to the plans of God for saving a lost humanity.

Whilst mission is important, it is not as important as the Church. In heaven there will be no mission because all God's people will already be gathered around the Lord and the Lamb (Revelation 5:9–14; 21:2–4). As Chris Green puts it, 'Mission is the means, not the end, but church is both the means and the end'.[73] The Puritans with their focus on heaven saw that and were motivated by that vision to be involved in passionate mission on earth. They had both heaven in their eye and earth on their heart.

7

Boston's Puritan credentials: Order in my chaotic world

The tiny rafts that Jim and I constructed didn't require maintenance, but now Jim sails boats that require a lot of maintenance. He has passed all his captains' exams and instructs as well as sails on the ocean. Facing the chaos and danger of the sea the ship must be properly maintained. The keel needs an annual check, cleaning and painting. The sails and rigging need to be regularly examined to keep them in perfect order. All the safety equipment and navigational stuff needs examining before setting off on a journey. Similarly the Christian life needs careful maintenance and order to face the dangers of the world, the flesh, and the devil so that progress towards Christian maturity can be kept going and the soul arrive safely in the haven of heaven. This is the fourth 'rope' on our imaginary raft.

Restoring man to his God-centred state

Before someone becomes a Christian he is in a fallen and

disordered condition. He is disordered because he does not
live according to the truth the mind is designed to get hold of.
His will operates by irrational feelings because he is not acting
according to the truth. His emotions are disordered because
they are meant to be led by a renewed mind acting as the
watchman of the soul. The Puritan John Owen develops this
idea by using Ecclesiastes 9:3, which shows the result of this
disordered condition: *madness in man all the days of his life.* We
see many examples of this in daily life. The teaching of the Bible
applied to the soul was designed by the Puritans to restore man
to a God-centric rather than egocentric condition. The enemies
of God will try and draw us back into chaos and disorder after
our conversion. God the Holy Spirit wars against the sinful
nature within us and no quarter is given because the two sides
are diametrically opposed to each other (Galatians 5:17). In
the swaying battle between the will of God and the rebellion
of the world, the flesh and the devil, each day is a day to be
won or lost for the Lord in the heart of the believer. And if we
have failed to walk according to the Spirit there is opportunity
for godly sorrow and the chance to start afresh with our hearts
sprinkled to cleanse us from a guilty conscience (Hebrews
10:22). A detailed study of this daily battle will be taken up
in the second section of this book on Richard Baxter, John
Bunyan and William Gurnall under the theme of the soldier-
pilgrim.

Order in my private and public world
I want to explore what Thomas Boston and the Puritans
have to teach us about a life of order in our work, play and
relationships. The Puritans took up the ideas of the monks of
the Middle-Ages and the teachers during the Patristic period

that the Christian life should be a life of order encompassing every aspect of life—work and rest, worship and relationships. The monks had lived and taught that to have an ordered life you needed to take yourself away to deserts and monasteries. Here in Cumbria and the North-East we have two famous monks, St Aidan and St Cuthbert, and several local churches are named after them. Bede says about Aidan that:

> the highest recommendation of his teaching to all was that he and his followers lived as they taught ... He never sought or cared for worldly possessions, and loved to give away whatever he received from kings or wealthy folk. He set himself to keep and teach the laws of God, and was diligent in study and in prayer.

Aidan's base was on the tidal island of Lindisfarne, now called Holy Island, which was the site of his monastery. The Puritans agreed with the monks about having an ordered life; not by retreating to monasteries but by living for Christ in the world whilst seeking to keep heaven in their eye and earth on their heart. They also did not think of the 'religious life' as the supreme form of Christian righteousness. In this they followed the Reformers like Luther, whose sermon on Matthew 22:34–46 taught that you don't have to undergo some monastic retreat or life apart from the world, you can bring glory to God by doing your daily tasks with a heart of love for God and for your neighbour:

> Therefore, what will happen on judgment day is that many a maidservant who did not know whether she had done anything good all her life will be preferred before a Carthusian monk

who has the appearance of great holiness and yet has loved neither God nor his neighbour. There God will pronounce this sentence: This maid has served her mistress in harmony with my commandment, has looked after the house, and so forth; since she has done this in faith, she shall be saved; but, Carthusian, you did what you wanted to do, serving no one but yourself and your own idol; therefore you are damned.[74]

Reformed monks

There is some justification in calling the Puritans 'reformed monks', a term used by Packer, because of their ordered lives. Of course they were different to monks in that they did not live in monasteries and they married and had children but the term is illuminating since in their concern for order they took up the monastic spirit. They lived in times when the world was in turmoil economically and politically, rather like our own times. In a world of chaos the man of God must establish order in his private world. In Book Three of Calvin's Institutes he taught principles for the godly life. The Puritans sought to follow Calvin's principles of the holy life: a detachment to one's commitments in the world, so that you do not lose yourself in them, and moderation in your enjoyments of the world, so you don't lose your heart in them and mistake earth for heaven. Only by following these principles will you be able to have order in your personal universe. Calvin warned against self-indulgence in the pleasures of the world, but on the other hand told us to enjoy the world as God's good gift to his children. This balanced approach was taken up by the Puritans.

Signs of true spiritual life

Order in your private world is one of the fruits of regeneration.

Thomas Boston writes about the effect of regeneration in the state of grace. He warns about mistaking partial changes for a great and thorough change. False conceptions can be found in the things of grace as well as nature and we need to take heed. For example, many may call the church their mother, he argues, but God will not own them as his children. Good education is not regeneration. A person may turn from open profanity but fall short of saving faith. A person may take part in all the outward forms and duties of religion and not be born again. Men may advance to a strict observance, as did Saul of Tarsus, and yet be strangers to the new birth. A person may even have 'soul-exercises and pangs, and yet die without grace'. Trees may blossom fairly in the spring on which no fruit is found in the harvest.

> ... There may be a wonderful moving of the affections in souls that are not at all touched with regenerating grace. When there is no grace, there may be, notwithstanding, be a flood of tears, as in Esau, who 'found no place of repentance, though he sought it carefully with tears' (Hebrews 12:17).[75]

Then Boston speaks of a real and thorough change and the signs of it in the believer. The old self is put off and the new self put on (Ephesians 4:22, 24), what he calls *a change of dispositions*. This is a supernatural change, whereby when we see a man so changed, we must say, *This is the finger of God*. Such change is into the likeness of God (Galatians 4:19). It is a universal change, when all things become new (2 Corinthians 5:17). He gets,

> not only a new head, to know and understand true religion:

or a new tongue, to talk of it; but a new heart, to love and
embrace it, in the whole of his life. When the Lord opens the
sluice of grace, on the soul's new-birth day, the waters run
through the whole man, to purify and make him fruitful.[76]

Although every part of the man is renewed there is no part of
him that is perfectly renewed. Just as an infant has available all
the parts of a man but none of them in perfect order, awaiting
growth to manhood, so is the believer. As newborn babes we
must desire the sincere milk of the word. In regeneration there
is light upon the mind, but there will be some darkness too.
Similarly with the will, it is not perfectly restored and part of
it will incline to sin until the day of deliverance. Whilst there
are these imperfections until heaven is reached, there is lasting
change,

> which never entirely dies off, since the seed is incorruptible.
> Whatever decays the seed remains in him who is born of God
> (1 John 3:9). Though the branches are cut back, the root abides
> in the earth and watered by the dew of heaven will grow again.[77]

How do you know you are regenerate?

The Puritans were in agreement among themselves that the fruit
of the Spirit is a new quality of life. If you have experienced
a real turning from sin to grace in your life this can give you
assurance by inference of a genuine and new quality of life
from God himself. That quality of life, said Boston and the
Puritans, will move you towards an ordered life where you get
control of your disordered world and bring God's order to it.
Part of that order was to keep heaven in your eye as you travel
on the narrow way to the celestial city. The Puritan's life will

be ordered to make sure he gets all that is needful: work, rest, and worship. By planning his life and exercising self-discipline, he will achieve order in his personal universe. By such means he will stay engaged in the world; but the world will not be mistaken for heaven because he will not lose himself in work or rest but his heart will continually be fixed on the worship of his God and the anticipation of heaven.

In 'The State of Grace: Regeneration', Boston outlines the impact of regeneration on the daily life. In the way of following his earthly business, there is great change, because now he has heaven in his eye and that affects every part of his life on earth:

> It appears to be no more his all, as it was before. Though saints apply themselves to worldly business, as well as others—yet their hearts are not swallowed up in it. It is evident that they are carrying on a trade with heaven, as well as a trade with earth, Philippians 3:20, 'For our conversation is in heaven.'[78]

A radical change of outlook

Saints do the same work but now they are not simply doing it for profit for themselves, but for heavenly profit to their souls and the souls of others. It may be mundane, repetitive work, but now they are doing it with their eyes on God and find pleasure in serving him in even humble tasks that take on a new significance because they are serving their loving Lord. In 'lawful comforts', Boston says there is a great change:

> They rest not in them, as their end; but use them as means to help them in their way. They draw their satisfaction from the higher springs—even while lower springs are running. Thus

Hannah, having obtained a son, rejoiced not so much in the gift, as in the giver, 1 Samuel 2:1, 'And Hannah prayed and said, My heart rejoices in the Lord.' Yes, when the comforts of life are gone, they can exist without them, and 'rejoice in the Lord although the fig-tree do not blossom,' Habbakuk 3:17–18.[79]

This is liberation from a total focus on this world alone, which will enable him to enjoy the world but know that this world will not bring lasting fulfilment. Aim at heaven and you will get earth thrown in. Aim at earth and you will get neither. 'Regenerating grace sets the affections so firmly on God, that the man is disposed, at God's command, to quit his hold of everything else, in order to keep his hold of Christ … It makes even lawful enjoyments, like Joseph's mantle, to hang loose about a man, that he might quit them, when he may be ensnared by holding them', says Boston.[80] In this sense the Christian can have a deeper enjoyment of the blessings of the world because he accepts them gratefully as gracious gifts from the Supreme Giver and lover of his soul. Even when these gifts are withdrawn or seasons of suffering come, the believer can still rejoice, because this situation will be temporary for testing and strengthening of the soul on the way to heaven, where all promises of blessing will be fulfilled and all suffering will cease.

Grace in relationships

In chapter five I raised the devastating critique of the Western church by Dallas Willard, when he points to a general worldliness of congregations where failures in the area of sex and money are joined by 'the presence of vanity, egoism, hostility, fear, indifference and downright meanness … amongst professing Christians'. This is prevalent in many churches, including evangelical ones, but what is the cause? Whilst God's people do 'err and stray like lost sheep' and we will always be 'a work in progress' this side of glory, genuine faith will reveal itself by transforming grace in relationships. Perhaps one cause of ungodly ministers and churches is because some folk in our churches, including some pastors have not experienced regeneration for themselves? An American pastor, Sam Storms, has written *What I Wish I'd Known: Ten Reflections on Nearly 40 Years of Pastoral Ministry.*[81]

> I wish I'd known about the destructive effects of insecurity in a pastor. This is less because I've struggled with it and more due to its effect I've seen in others. Why is insecurity so damaging?

> • Insecurity makes it difficult to acknowledge and appreciate the accomplishments of others on staff (or in the congregation). In other words, the personally insecure pastor is often incapable of offering genuine encouragement to others. Their success becomes a threat to him, his authority, and his status in the eyes of the people. Thus if you're insecure you likely won't pray for others to flourish.

> • Insecurity will lead a pastor to encourage and support and praise another pastor only insofar as the latter serves the former's agenda and doesn't detract from his image.

> • An insecure pastor will likely resent the praise or affirmation other staff members receive from the people at large.

> • For the insecure pastor, constructive criticism is not received well, but is perceived as a threat or outright rejection.

- Because the insecure pastor is incapable of acknowledging personal failure or lack of knowledge, he's often unteachable. He will resist those who genuinely seek to help him or bring him information or insights he lacks. His spiritual growth is therefore stunted.

- The insecure pastor is typically heavy-handed in his dealings with others.

- The insecure pastor is often controlling and given to micromanagement.

- The insecure pastor rarely empowers or authorizes others to undertake tasks for which they're especially qualified and gifted. He won't release others but rather restrict them.

- The insecure pastor is often given to outbursts of anger.

- At its core, insecurity is the fruit of pride.

In summary, and at its core, insecurity results from not believing the gospel. The antidote to feelings of insecurity, then, is the rock-solid realization that one's value and worth are in the hands of God, not others, and that our identity expresses who we are in Christ. Only as we deepen our grasp of his sacrificial love for us will we find the liberating confidence to affirm and support others without fearing their successes or threats.

This is Sam Storms final point in his list of ten things and it's by far the longest! Like Sam it's not something I've particularly experienced but I have seen its destructive effect in others. I think his list of ten things goes a long way in addressing Dallas Willard's point in chapter five about ungodly ministers and congregations. It is regeneration and an ongoing experience of the grace of God expressed in daily repentance that leads to transformation into Christlikeness in relationships. Without it we will live according to the world and not according to heaven! To live this way is to lose heaven and gain a place in hell instead.

Marriage for the Puritans

Marriage is the basic unit of human order in society and brings order to life. The Bible tells us how husband and wife and children and parents should relate to one another. The Puritans gave us the Christian home as an ideal to aspire to. They put in a lot of time encouraging fathers, mothers and children to love one another. It is an institution for the good and blessing of all of society and yet this current U.K. government is intent on undermining it by the redefinition of marriage to include gay couples. This will only create more gender confusion and weaken family life which is based on heterosexual monogamy.

The Puritans gave excellent advice about choosing a wife or husband. Look at the inner beauty of the person not just the physical attraction, they advised. This outlook comes from the perspective of heaven because this beauty will last in eternity whilst earthly beauty will fade away (Proverbs 31:30 says, 'Charm is deceitful, and beauty is vain, but a woman who fears the Lord is to be praised'). Look for someone to marry said the Puritans you think you will still admire in fifty years time, rather than just having a temporary infatuation. Take advice from your parents and wider family and friends and do not be hasty. Choose, as Scripture says, someone who knows and loves the Lord Jesus as you do. You are looking to a long future together, forming a secure home in which to bring up your children in the Lord.

The marriage service was usually in a church building for the Puritans and normally included a substantial sermon from the Bible. My younger daughter got married in 2010; I was privileged to lead the ceremony and another minister preached a good sermon. In my own married life I have taken seriously the role of being the head of the family and having the responsibility to serve and love my wife and teach my children about God. I am grateful to God that both our daughters are following the Lord and our younger daughter has married a keen Christian man. The Puritans had the idea of the home as being a little church and a little commonwealth. This was a powerful thought in the 16th and 17th century since the family was a little church for godliness and a little commonwealth for order. Sadly, the Christian family that the Puritans bequeathed to us is under great threat today but where there are good churches teaching the living word of God, strong Christian families can still be built.

Heaven in your eye must come first

We have seen how the Puritans had a comprehensive view of life that covered work, marriage and the family, rest and worship which brought order to their lives. Boston taught that you should be heavenly-minded, no matter how much you are concentrating on the tasks of this world. You can give your all to them but not your soul which belongs to God in heaven where he waits to greet your arrival. The Puritans avoided the trap of believing you will be saved by obeying your minister in everything he says, but instead relied upon the freedom of your own conscience, which they were encouraged to make a servant to the word of God. Everyday life in Puritan times was chaotic but through discipline you could bring order to your private world. Each day on earth would be a battle. We will see more about this daily struggle in the final chapter of this section about Boston's battles and in the next section on Richard Baxter and John Bunyan, soldier-pilgrims.

Boston's Puritan credentials: Battles on the way to heaven

We have seen what a great shepherd-captain Boston was in terms of the legacy to the church of his helpful theological paradigm contained in the *Fourfold State* and his faithful pastoral and preaching ministry in his small parishes in Scotland. But what about Boston contending for the faith that was once for all delivered to the saints (Jude 3)? Some minsters are happy to be warm pastoral men but lack the backbone for the fight. Was Boston such a man? Whilst we have seen that Boston shared the Puritan concern for holiness to the Lord in church and state, did that lead to his involvement in theological controversy or did he just keep to his quiet backwater? Consideration of Boston's battles will lead us naturally in the next section of the book to consider the question of Puritan warfaring in more detail around the issue of the 'Great Ejection' of 1662, looked at from the point of view of three representative Puritans: Baxter, Bunyan and Gurnall. Whilst Boston fulfils the

first four characteristics of the Puritans did he fulfil the one of
contending for the faith, the fifth 'rope' on our imaginary raft?

Our analogy of the raft comes to an end in this chapter but
not the connection to my brother Jim who, aged eighteen,
signed on to the army and rose to the rank of sergeant in
the Royal Signals. This gave him discipline to his life as
well as providing a great foundation for his later career in
telecommunications in the banking world and an opportunity
to develop his love of sailing by looking after the company
yacht. Our parents always thought I would join the army
because of my childhood love of playing with toy soldiers on
the living room floor, but it was not to be. When it comes
to Boston he was not a natural soldier-pilgrim since he had
a timid disposition and suffered constant physical infirmity
and depression throughout his life. Nonetheless in true New
Testament and Puritan fashion he embraced a life of spiritual
warfare which was very costly since it went against the grain
of his natural life. In this he demonstrated that he was a true
Puritan.

In this chapter we will consider Boston's spiritual battles
set against his human weakness and how through union with
Christ Boston prevailed in his struggles. Such 'strength in
weakness' will be of great value in developing the emotional
resilience a Christian needs when faced by the pressures of
gospel ministry. Boston and other Puritans can help us form
that 'cultivated heart, assisted by the grace of God' as Dallas
Willard describes it that can overcome great setbacks and keep
going faithfully to the end of our lives. I say *lives*, because
simply 'retiring' from paid work either in the church or the

world does not mean an end to Christian ministry but simply a transfer to other fields of opportunity for service. There is no retirement from the Kingdom of God for the true Christian. I will deal with this subject more fully in chapter thirteen.

1. A Timid Nature and God's provision

Boston was not by temperament a fighter. I have known many good men in the ministry who have exercised their work conscientiously but yet have avoided all forms of confrontation. By inclination Boston would have been very comfortable taking such an approach but he was driven by his love of Christ to speak up.

'The first Sabbath I preached, being timorous, I had not confidence to look on the people; though I do believe I did not close my eyes'.[82] He writes that, God 'so pitied his natural weakness that once the pulpit door was closed on me, fear was as it were closed out; and I feared not the face of man when preaching God's word'. It was his deep sense of union with Christ that gave him this confidence, as he writes that, 'I esteem Christ above all: Give me Christ, and take from me what thou wilt'.

God also provided a wife that was suitable for him:

What engaged me to her, was her piety, parts, beauty, cheerful disposition fitted to temper mine, and that I reckoned her very fit to see to my health.[83]

My own testimony would echo that of Boston and as the writer of Proverbs expresses it, 'House and wealth are inherited from fathers, but a prudent wife is from the Lord' (Proverbs 19:14). Boston's wife clearly had some medical skill, hence his comment that *I reckoned her very fit to see to my health*. My wife has the same inclination and skill, being a nurse! As I write this, my wife is travelling to London by train to help our daughter with our first grandson and I have just sent her a text including the above quote from Boston about his wife, applying it to her and our very happy marriage.

A desire for heaven and a great struggle

All the Puritans speak of a swaying battle with evil, which is part of the cosmic battle between God and the world, the flesh and the devil:

> Reflecting on how faithful God has been in answering his prayers in the midst of great struggle with a sense of fear, Boston exclaims, 'But how will I get through the world? Happy are they that are in heaven'. Soon afterwards, feeling that his feet had almost slipped (Psalm 73:2), he declares that 'Satan set on again with the same; but I cried to the Lord, and he fled'.[84]

Boston knew that combat that Paul writes about in Ephesians 6 and what William Gurnall discussed in his classic *The Christian In Complete Armour*. In the next section we will look at this swaying battle in more detail, but suffice it to say that in spite of a natural reluctance on the part of many ministers to join such a struggle it is part of the minister's calling and Boston was not lacking in spiritual zeal, even if his natural self was weak. We would all do well to remember that both the Lord Jesus and the Apostle Paul were controversialists. We must strive to be as gracious as possible but inevitably we will cause offence and opposition because the gospel itself will cause such a reaction. Paul addresses the temptation of being ashamed or timid by speaking of the power of the gospel to save people and transform them by God's grace (Romans 1:16 and 2 Timothy 1:7). Boston had developed a 'cultivated heart, assisted by the grace of God', and this enabled him to consistently engage in spiritual warfare. Boston keeps in his mind, 'Happy are they that are in heaven'. In other words this battle will not last for ever. One day the saints will cease their warfare against sin because in heaven they will be in a state of glory where sin is no more.

2. Physical infirmity and perseverance

Boston was subject to constant ailments and physical struggles, yet he was able to say in his autobiography that he had not failed to preach on each Sabbath, during his thirty year ministry. In spite of his physical weakness he covered the hundred square miles of his parish on horseback, visiting each of his families for spiritual check-up and encouragement. In his first eight years at Simprin, amongst what he called 'his handful', he confessed to his wife to feeling no great warmth for the people in his charge but he persevered until God sent his blessing on the work. This was in spite of his physical struggles:

'The binding at my breast had returned, and I was seized with pains in my back, and in the hinder part of my head, so that I began to apprehend my time in the world might not be long: and on that occasion I found I had some evidences for a better world, and was somewhat submissive to the divine disposal'.[85]

His description of preaching in great weakness is reminiscent of Paul speaking of the *thorn in his flesh* and God teaching him about *strength in weakness* (2 Corinthians 12:9):

'I was pressed with a sense of my insufficiency for that work, that heaven was very desirable for me'.[86]

Heaven is constantly in Boston's eye because in heaven that sense of frustration and weakness will be removed, but in the meantime the battle is unrelenting. Concerned that *the devil should not pick up the seed sown*, Boston shows disappointment at the response of the people to his sermon in that 'several of them told me of the earthly part, but quite forgot the heavenly part'.[87]

This is such a common experience of parish ministry where the parable of the soils is such an accurate description of the response of many to ardent faithful preaching. We need to keep scattering the seed of the word, knowing that the good soil will produce an abundant crop in God's time. We must realise that we are in a battle and that we will face opposition even from the people we are trying to help. Paul says, 'the god of this world has blinded the minds of the unbelievers, to keep them from seeing the light of the gospel of the glory of Christ, who is the image of God' (2 Corinthians 4:4).

This swaying battle with sin and Satan appears regularly in Boston's journal:

Ah for the power and prevalency of unbelief! I think if there were no more in heaven but freedom from this master-devil, it were most desirable.[88]

He echoes Paul's desire: 'My desire is to depart and be with Christ, for that is far better. But to remain in the flesh is more necessary on your account' (Philippians 1:23–24), when he writes in his journal that:

> Had I one wish, it should be, that he would wrap me up in his love, light, and life, while I am here, and take me away to eternity when he pleased, though I would fain do something for Christ here.[89]

This expresses the Puritan and New Testament approach to heaven and earth: a desire to be with Christ, 'which is far better'; but also a desire to be useful to Christ and to people on earth.

Throughout he confesses the struggle with his old nature:

> I am amazed at the baseness of my heart ... and am many times afraid my religion is of the wrong stamp.[90]

On the other hand, he constantly refers to heaven, using phrases such as these:

> Admiring heaven as a place of rest from sin; I was somewhat heavenly; my heart being heavenly; a heavenly frame of spirit; a little heaven to me; a heavenly disposition

and he frequently speaks of 'looking upward to heaven'.

Equally there are numerous references to 'the baseness of his heart', the fact that 'I am surrounded by evils on every hand' and 'O the deceit of Satan'. This shows the reality of the spiritual forces arrayed against God's people.

Such candid comments from the heart of such a faithful minister of the gospel who felt great weakness and yet through union with Christ felt the power of the Holy Spirit empowering his life is so encouraging. Boston's hope of heaven was critical for his spiritual progress in spite of natural weakness. It helped him to overcome his tendency to morbidity. Martyn Lloyd-Jones, a former doctor, has a chapter in his book *Spiritual Depression* based on Psalm 42, which I have found very helpful when tempted to despair. He encourages us to think carefully about our constitution and also to consider our circumstances whilst echoing the Psalmist's diagnostic question, 'Why are you downcast my soul?' Ultimately there is the light at the end of the tunnel because of the hope of heaven the gospel offers, no matter how long the tunnel may be! I have been inspired to help others go through the dark night of the soul by reading of the great support and care John Newton gave to his friend and fellow hymn-writer William Cowper, who attempted to take his own life several times because of severe depression but the kind and patient Newton helped him to recovery on each occasion.

3. Struggling with depression and a sick wife

Throughout his life Boston struggled with severe depression:

> I am habitually cast down, and cannot win to get my heart lifted up in the ways of the Lord ... I am a melancholy fool ... many a heavy and melancholy day have I had, though various causes and occasions ... No religion was left me now, but a

sorrowful looking up to the Lord, whom I had provoked to withdraw.[91]

But then Boston begins to see a bit of light dawning when he preaches and gets 'a good deal of serenity of mind'. I have found myself that when I preach the word of God it does lift me out of my sometimes despairing circumstances and feelings, provided I preach the word to myself first and then to others.

Shortly afterwards we see the answer to Boston' prayers, as he recounts that,

> The Lord in the morning began to blow on my soul, and continue so to do … and with all willingness of soul I renewed and subscribed a personal covenant with God … my heart was calmed and strengthened in the Lord, and my mind made heavenly.[92]

Keeping spiritual journals and making personal covenants was the Puritan way of keeping an account of this swaying battle and recounting not just the struggles and failures but the constant love and providence of God in response to the saints' cries for help. At the end of this particular struggle, Boston writes in his journal:

> My soul was filled with praises and admiration of the Lord's kindness to poor me at this juncture, notwithstanding my woeful backslidings from Him before. O the doctrine of the gospel, and revelation of Christ, is sweet to my soul. I have felt strength against corruption this day.[93]

On the occasion of his marriage on the 17th July 1700 to Catherine Brown he recounts that 'the Lord filled my heart with joy in Himself unspeakable' and having likened his wife to the woman of Proverbs 31, concludes that 'during the time we have lived together hitherto, we have passed through a sea of trouble'.[94] As well as the pressures of ministry and the sad loss of two children, Boston also faced dealing with the mental illness of his wife in later years. In spite of these struggles he concludes in his autobiography written to encourage his children to follow the Lord that,

> And now for the third part of the time we have lived together, *namely ten years complete, she has been under a particular* racking distress; and for several of these years, fixed to her bed; in which furnace, the grace of God in her hath brightened.[95]

4. Battling for the purity of the gospel

Boston admits that he was 'much addicted to peace, and averse to controversy; though once engaged therein, I was set to go through with it'.[96] Boston was involved in two main controversies. The first concerned Professor John Simpson who was accused of undermining the incarnation of Christ in his teaching ministry. The Kirk agreed that Simpson was guilty but was not willing to suspend him from office. Boston stood alone in calling for this action to be carried out due to the seriousness of Simpson's offences. Whilst Thomas Boston was a retiring sort of personality, he was prepared to overcome his natural reticence and exhibited a zero tolerance of false teaching. In the introduction to Boston's autobiography George H. Morrison describes the unpopular stance Boston took to the Kirk's indulgence of serious theological error:

Boston like Athanasius stood alone. Boston was clear that if
the charges had been proven, Simpson should be deposed. He
could not tolerate the unfaithful gentleness of the Assembly.[97]

This is a similar statement to Luther regarding what he
termed, *sinful silence.* A great temptation for all Christians is to
remain silent when we should speak up. We stay silent hoping
that the false teaching will simply go away! But false teaching is
very dangerous because it will draw people away, to the loss of
their souls. To remain silent in such circumstances is not loving
(see Paul's warning to the Ephesian elders in Acts 20:28–31). I
am reminded of the lone figure of Revd David Holloway, Vicar
of Jesmond parish in Newcastle protesting at the consecration
of David Jenkins as Bishop of Durham at York Minster in 1984
because Jenkins had publicly denied the bodily resurrection of
Jesus. Perhaps some saw David Holloway's stance as harsh but
he was right to protest and so was Boston.

The second matter of controversy concerned the book *The
Marrow of Modern Divinity* written by an Englishman Edward
Fisher. In George H. Morrison's introduction to the 1899
edition of Boston's autobiography,[98] he describes *The Marrow*
as no dry compend[ium] of theology. It is the earnest effort of
a Christian and a scholar to solve some of the problems of his
time. It is the endeavour of a 'middle man' to take the 'middle
path', and the middle path, the only way to heaven, says Boston
in his note 'was Jesus Christ truly received by faith, and walked
in answerably by holiness of heart and life'. Fisher addressed the
point of strain in the system of covenant theology between the
covenants of law and grace. Fisher had struggled for twelve years
with legalism, ignorant of the secret of free grace. Then the light

had dawned and he outlined his findings in *The Marrow*, which Boston discovered in one of the cottages of Simprin and found liberating to his soul.

Boston had been greatly helped to hold to free grace by *The Marrow* and sought to promote it amongst his friends. However, there were complaints that the book encouraged antinomianism [*nomian* means law] and it was banned by the Assembly of the Church of Scotland. Boston and twelve of his friends tried to have this ban lifted but were unsuccessful and ended up being censured for giving the book their support. In 1722 Boston and the 'Marrow men' were 'admonished and rebuked' for their support of *The Marrow*, but no more action was taken against them.

In these matters the Church of Scotland showed its inability to follow a middle path of grace and truth between the two dangers of liberalism, in the Professor John Simpson case, and legalism in the Marrow Controversy. Ryken thinks that these two decisions reveal the theological weakness of the Church of Scotland of the day. This view coincides with Boston's own assessment at the time:

> One prevalent view, a view which echoes Boston's own interpretation of events maintains that the 'severity' with which the Marrow and its defenders were treated stands in marked contrast to the leniency of John Simpson's sentence ... [and indicates] that the majority of those who made up the Church of Scotland, 'more inclined to countenance error than to defend the truth'.[99]

The Church of Scotland of Boston's day failed to follow a middle path of grace and truth and it is showing the same tendencies today by embracing acceptance of the gay lifestyle amongst clergy and laity. Already several large evangelical fellowships have been forced to leave the Church of Scotland and others may follow.

Homosexuality A Minor Issue?

Many folk have taken this approach, wrongly in my view. Indulgences in Luther's time were a relatively minor issue but underneath represented the major error of salvation by works. Luther and others had to get back to the Scriptures and stand upon the truth of justification by faith alone, through Christ alone. They likened the error to that of the Pharisees of Jesus' time. I know some like Tom Wright have suggested that Luther and the Reformers were labouring under a false understanding of Judaism but many have refuted such theories, including John Piper. Some today suggest that the homosexuality issue is either not clear in the Bible or is not that critical (see *The Bible and Homosexual Practice* by Robert A. J. Gagnon to see how these views are refuted). The fact is that the revisionism behind the drive within the church to accept homosexual practice as godly does not reflect the Bible's teaching that it is clearly sinful (see 1 Corinthians 6:9 and Romans 1:24–27). It is appropriate to say here, to be clear, that anyone homosexual or heterosexual living a life-style that is contrary to the Bible will not be saved. Being homosexual will not send you to hell but living an unrepentant homosexual lifestyle will certainly do so.

For a federation of local churches to affirm its support for what the Bible so clearly condemns will lead to the demise of those churches. This has been seen in the catastrophic decline of the Episcopal Church in the United States since it accepted this false teaching. For the Church of Scotland to embrace this teaching must inevitably result in the decline of the Church of Scotland that Boston loved. If the Church of England adopts this revisionist agenda and turns its back on the Thirty-Nine Articles, the Ordinal and other formularies, then it will also see irreversible decline and have its candlestick removed by the Lord Jesus (see Revelation 2:5).

Archbishop Eliud Wabukala, Primate of Kenya and Chairman of the GAFCON Primates' Council wrote in July 2013 that the Jerusalem Statement of 2008 had spoken prophetically of three 'undeniable facts':

1. 'The acceptance and promotion within the provinces of the Anglican Communion of a different "gospel".'

2. 'The declaration by provincial bodies in the Global South that they are out of communion with bishops and churches that promote this false gospel.'

3. 'The manifest failure of the Communion Instruments (its international institutions) to exercise discipline in the face of overt heterodoxy.'

This shows that a large part of the Anglican Communion do not see the revisionist agenda expressed by the acceptance of homosexual practice as a minor issue but as another gospel that must be opposed (see Galatians 1:6).

As we have seen, Boston was not a controversialist by nature like another great Scottish Christian leader, John Knox; in fact Boston was a shy man who suffered from bodily weakness and bouts of depression. However, he was so motivated by his consciousness of eternity and winning or losing heaven that he was willing, in great weakness, to speak out on earth. If he was alive today he would be warning the Church of Scotland about hitting the rocks of moral and spiritual error in its acceptance of homosexual genital acts. He would do so with grace and truth. He would be reluctant to get involved in controversy but having joined the fray he would '*set to go through with it*'. We too must accept that holding on to and holding out the gospel will mean facing up to opposition and false teaching with grit, grace and truth as Boston did. If such a weak man by constitution could stand up for truth then every minister and every lay person can also do so. Let us put aside our excuses and when the situation demands speak up clearly and winsomely for the truth revealed in the Scriptures, even if it is costly to do so. Boston was willing to 'fight the good fight of faith' and so should we.

Section Two:
Soldier-Pilgrims

9

1662: Missed opportunities and tragedy for the Church of England

In this section we will focus on the issue of the 'Church Militant'. In this chapter we will ask what *Heaven in Your Eye and Earth on Your Heart* did for three English Puritans who in 1662 made entirely different responses to the key question of: 'What shall I do about the Church of England?' These Puritans were Richard Baxter, John Bunyan and William Gurnall. Each of them is a classic example of the soldier-pilgrim willing to battle for the gospel. This story is not just relevant to faithful Anglicans but also to non-conformists and Free Church folk facing the same battles to be true to Scripture today. The biblical raft of security that sustained Boston also enabled Bunyan, Baxter and Gurnall to survive the severe storms of their lives and prove the truth of Dallas Willard's claim that 'A carefully cultivated heart will, assisted by the grace of God, foresee, forestall, or transform most of the painful situations before which others stand like helpless children saying "Why?"'

We will also see once again that the transforming paradox that C. S. Lewis states is also true of these three Puritans: *Aim at heaven and you will get earth 'thrown in': aim at earth and you will get neither.*

J. I. Packer sums up the importance of spiritual struggle for the Puritans when he writes:

> Spiritual warfare made the Puritans what they were. They accepted conflict as their calling, seeing themselves as their Lord's soldier-pilgrims, just as in Bunyan's allegory, and not expecting to be able to advance a single step without opposition of one sort or another.[100]

The Circumstances of the Great Ejection of 1662

Oliver Cromwell died in 1658. His son Richard was made Protector but was unable to rule as his father did. Charles the son of the executed King was very keen to win widespread support for the return of the monarchy and made extravagant promises to the religious groups, including the Puritans at *The Declaration at Breda* in April 1660, that there would be general religious toleration and all groups would have freedom of conscience within a newly constituted Church of England. Charles was given support from the Puritan and Presbyterian parties to become King. Unfortunately, when he was installed as King he went back on these promises. The Laudian group (followers of the executed Archbishop of Canterbury, William Laud) had been with Charles during his exile and were determined to exclude the Puritans from the Church of England and pass laws that would persecute those unwilling to agree to their Act of Conformity. This Act also applied to political office and so it alienated a great section of English society for a hundred and fifty years.

The Act was to come into force on St Bartholomew's Day, when many French Protestants had been executed by the Catholic French King Louis XIV. It was intended to destroy Puritan influence in the Church of England. Ministers had to agree that they would not take up arms against the King and would follow a series of liturgical practices that many Puritans found unacceptable: wearing the surplice, signing the cross at baptism and kneeling at communion. The ruling party in the Church of England wanted to make it impossible for the Puritans to stay within the Church of England and they largely succeeded. They chose to enact the bill on this day so that they would deprive the Puritan ministers of the tithes and glebe payments they were to get later in the year as part of their stipend. This was a malicious and disastrous act by a group determined to get revenge on the Puritans for their part in the execution of Charles the First and the years of the Protectorate under Oliver Cromwell, when many of them had been exiled abroad.

Three different Puritan responses to the crisis of 1662

1. John Bunyan: Independent
John Bunyan chose to leave his local parish church and support independency after his conversion. He grew up in a time of great trouble in the church and nation that led to a bitter and terrible civil war. He fought on the Parliamentary side in the civil war and was therefore naturally aligned with the religious

dissenters against the official tax-supported church, the Church of England. With the restoration of the Monarch he would suffer persecution over his refusal to attend his Anglican parish church and his persistence in preaching without a licence and as a consequence spent ten years in Bedford jail. Later on we will look at the writings that were the fruit of his incarceration, particularly *Pilgrims Progress* and *The Heavenly Footman.*

Bunyan's view of the Church of England was that he wanted to be entirely free of it! He denounced the Church of England as false and he vowed never to attend Anglican services. Bunyan's *A Relation of My Imprisonment,* published posthumously in 1765 contained a transcript of his trial October 3, 1660, which led to his imprisonment at Bedford,

> Judge Wingate: 'Mr. Bunyan, you stand before this Court accused of persistent and willful transgression of the Conventicle Act, which prohibits all British subjects from absenting themselves from worship in the Church of England, and from conducting worship services apart from our Church ... I hold in my hand the depositions of the witnesses against you. In each case, they have testified that, to their knowledge, you have never, in your adult life, attended services in the Church of this parish. Each further testifies that he has observed you, on numerous occasions, conducting religious exercises in and near Bedford.'

> John Bunyan: 'The depositions speak the truth. I have never attended services in the Church of England, nor do I intend ever to do so. Secondly, it is no secret that I preach the Word of God whenever, wherever, and to whomever He pleases to grant me opportunity to do so. I have no choice but to acknowledge

my awareness of the law which I am accused of transgressing. Likewise, I have no choice but to confess my guilt in my transgression of it. As true as these things are, I must affirm that I neither regret breaking the law, nor repent of having broken it. Further, I must warn you that I have no intention in the future of conforming to it.'

Judge Wingate: 'It is obvious, sir, that you are a victim of deranged thinking. If my ears deceive me not, I must infer from your words that you believe the State to have no interest in the religious life of its subjects.'

John Bunyan: 'The State, my lord, may have an interest in anything in which it wishes to have an interest. But the State has no right whatever to interfere in the religious life of its citizens.'[101]

This was Bunyan's position and he was prepared to suffer the loss of his freedom and even death if necessary because of his views. If he had agreed to attend his parish church and stop preaching he could have walked free. Instead he suffered for his stand regarding freedom of religion. I do not share his particular views on the Prayer Book and Episcopacy but I defend his right to hold them and to seek to worship God according to his conscience. Bunyan was adamantly opposed to Anglicanism.

Bunyan thought the prayer book and Episcopacy were tainted by Roman Catholicism and must be totally rejected.

A good sense of sin, and the wrath of God, with some encouragement from God to come to him, is a better prayer-book than that which is taken out of the Roman Catholic mass-book, which are nothing but the scraps and fragments of the inventions of some popes, monks, and who knows what else ... When David felt the 'cords of death entangle [him], and the anguish of the grave coming upon [him],' he did not need a bishop dressed in a fancy robe to teach him to say, 'O Lord, save me!' (Psalm 116:3, 4). Nor did he need to look into a book, to teach him a form of a prayer to pour out before God.[102]

Bunyan had no time for denominational labels either.

As for those titles of Anabaptists, Independents, Presbyterians, or the like, I conclude that they come neither from Jerusalem nor from Antioch, but rather from hell and Babylon, for they naturally tend to division.[103]

But was Bunyan just a dissenter uninterested in the unity of the living church? No, I don't think so. Whilst Bunyan did believe in believer's baptism there is evidence that he did not insist upon it for church membership.

While generally characterized by the belief that adult baptism, the baptism of believers should be the condition of reception into the church, Baptists in Seventeenth Century England were a diverse group ... John Bunyan belonged to the open-communion group Baptist Church, which was also Calvinist in theology, but did not insist on the necessity of adult baptism.[104]

Bunyan's views on the 1662 Ejection

Bunyan would have seen the 1662 ejection as a good thing in that two thousand godly Puritans left an unholy church and were forced into non-conformity. In Bunyan's case he chose that out of conscience.

I will deal with Baxter and Gurnall more briefly here in regard to the 1662 ejection. Both were Episcopalians but one decided in good conscience he could not agree to the Act of Uniformity and left, whilst the other decided he could in good conscience agree and stayed in the Church of England. Both suffered for their decisions, made in good faith and no doubt after much thought and struggle.

2. Richard Baxter: reluctant non-conformist

Baxter shot to fame after writing his first book, *The Saints Everlasting Rest* about heaven. A chaplain in Cromwell's model army he became seriously ill as a result of sleeping in the fields and thought he was dying. We will consider *The Saints Everlasting Rest* later and also his book on the renewal of the Church called *The Reformed Pastor*. We will confine our discussion to what impact Baxter's idea of heaven had on his books and on his life. Although he rose to prominence in the Puritan party, he had reservations about the execution of Charles I, and was involved in the Restoration of the monarchy. Offered a bishopric, he decided instead to leave the Church of England because he could not in conscience give support to the Act of Uniformity. Like Bunyan, his subsequent life was a life of constant hardship and persecution. Was he right to leave? Several Puritans were offered bishoprics and senior positions. If they had all stayed perhaps they could have made the conditions of the Act of Uniformity acceptable to a greater number of Puritans. This is very difficult to ascertain. Lee Gatiss tells us that,

Baxter, Reynolds, and Calamy were offered bishoprics and other leading puritans proposed for important preferment. Yet they did not all accept (Reynolds did but Baxter and Calamy declined).[105]

Perhaps Baxter and the others could have made a difference, we don't know. What we do know is Baxter made the judgment that nothing could be achieved by staying and took the hard road of being a high-profile dissenter, drawing upon himself some disgraceful treatment from despicable people like Judge Jefferies who not only sent Baxter to prison and confiscated his books but also wanted to take his bed from him! This was only prevented by the intervention of John Owen making a plea for clemency to the King, which was granted. Baxter made his judgment on what to do and we must afford him respect. What we also know, with hindsight, is that the removal of two thousand of the best Puritan ministers was a disaster for the Church of England for the next hundred and fifty years and has left a legacy of non-conformity ever since.

3. William Gurnall: reluctant conformist

William Gurnall was the author of the popular Puritan book, *The Christian In Complete Armour*. His story is just as fascinating as the better known story of Baxter and Bunyan for the lack of information we have about him. We know only four things: That he was a Puritan divine in the seventeenth century; that he wrote a well-known book of practical religion; that he was Vicar of Lavenham; and that he signed the Act of Uniformity and was re-ordained by Bishop Reynolds. Why we have so little information available to us is a matter of conjecture but we can suggest a possible answer. It is likely that very little was written about him because of his decision to support the infamous Act of Uniformity in 1662. We do know that there were tracts written by fellow Puritans denouncing this decision and this may afford us a reason to explain the lack of historical information.

What can we learn from 1662?

Bunyan's view of the Church of England would be held by many present-day non-conformists. Gary Brady takes a typical Reformed Baptist view in *1662 The Great Ejection.*[106]

> The Puritans tried for more than a hundred years to work within the Church of England. In 1662 the majority of them felt compelled to say enough is enough and so they were ejected ... The Anglican church of today is undoubtedly very different to what it was in 1662, though not all things have changed. Anyone who chooses to work within it ought to be aware of its history.

This view follows the logic of Martyn Lloyd-Jones whom Gary Brady quotes a good deal, who advocated a wholesale exit of conservative evangelicals from the Church of England in the 1960s because it was a mixed church. John Stott a close friend of Lloyd-Jones refused to do so and encouraged men to stay and fight for its reform. Who was right, Stott or Lloyd-Jones? Whilst there have been many setbacks there have also been notable gains according to J. I. Packer, who was a good friend of both men. Writing in VirtueOnline Packer looks at Bishop Ryle and Charles Simeon (both prominent Anglican evangelical leaders) and suggests that both of them would encourage evangelical Anglicans to stay and fight within the Church of England rather than leaving the struggling ship. Packer says that from what we know of them they would ask us to consider five things:

(1) We should remember that the defined faith, the historical heritage and the calling, evangelistic pastoral and prophetic, of the English national church remain what they were, despite the incursion of tolerated errors;

(2) We should realise that the 'guilt by association' argument touches no one who explicitly dissociates himself from the errors concerned;

(3) We should remind ourselves that by leaving the Church of England in disgust at its doctrinal disorders we should stand to lose more than we gained;

(4) We should regard these errors, which are all well-meant efforts to restate the faith for today, in terms of deficiency—failure, that is, for whatever reason, to affirm the full gospel—and devote energy to filling in what they omit or refuse to say;

(5) We should recognize that the best way to serve a church infected by error is to refute the error cogently in public discussion and debate, as Paul refuted the Galatian and Colossian errors, and Athanasius the Arian error, and Augustine the Pelagian error, and Luther Erasmus' semi-Pelagianism.[107]

On the same website Packer poses the question, 'Can you in good conscience choose to be an Anglican Minister today?' This is his answer:

I maintain that a man with his eyes open to the full range of Anglican doctrinal pluralism may yet responsibly choose to be an Anglican, even an Anglican minister, though it may be a hard-made decision bringing misery as well as fulfilment. I do not maintain (I had better say this outright) that choosing to be an Anglican is a virtue, or that choosing not to be one or not to stay one is a vice. Choice, we saw, is necessary, and anyone may conclude that, rather than be Anglican, Methodist, Baptist Union or United Reformed (all which bodies are doctrinally mixed), he should join one of the smaller groups (Brethren, Pentecostals, Fellowship of Independent Evangelical Churches, Reformed Baptists, Free Church of Scotland, etc.) which debar from the ranks of their teachers anyone holding 'critical' views of Scripture or rejecting major evangelical tenets. To be sure, some think these smaller bodies purchase doctrinal purity at the price of theological stagnation, and are cultural backwaters out of touch with society around, just as some think Anglican allegiance is an unholy identification with cultural privilege, ecclesiastical worldliness and theological indifferentism. But these matters are arguable both ways, and neither estimate need be accepted. More important is respect for the other man's deliberate decision, whether or not it coincides with your own.[108]

Packer's concluding remark about mutual respect for fellow evangelicals goes to the heart of what is to be learnt from the tragedy of 1662. Each of the three Puritans we are considering took a very different course of action to the crisis in the church. Bunyan made his response to the religious situation of his day in good conscience and with great courage. Having heaven in his eye emboldened him to risk all for conscience's sake and take the position of an independent. We have seen already that Baxter and Gurnall took completely different approaches from Bunyan to the Church of England. All three were sustained in the circumstances they found themselves in by knowing they had followed their consciences, and were empowered to suffer through their humble hope of heaven.

Conservative evangelicals should give each other mutual respect and support.

Speaking of the relationship between different Puritans Lee Gatiss comments that, 'There should perhaps have been much greater unity in practice between those Anglicans, Presbyterians, Independents, and Baptists who agreed on the foundational tenets of the faith'.[109]

In chapter five I referred to the Leith Anderson's very helpful assessment of contemporary church life, which ends with this conclusion:

> Those who strive to be New Testament churches must seek to
> live its principles and absolutes, not produce the details.

Heaven in our eye should remind us today that we belong together and we will be together with the Lord in heaven. In the stormy waters to come we should allow each other to make decisions based on conscience and seek to keep the unity of the spirit in the bond of peace. We can try to learn from history to make the main thing the main thing. Whatever course we take we will need *a cultivated heart, assisted by the grace of God.* Heaven in our eye and earth on our heart will certainly make a key contribution to our sense of security and well-being as we exercise humble hope under pressure. I sometimes joke with my congregation that perhaps there might be seminars in heaven! Maybe one discussion point might be to consider which Puritan group was right, since they were split. What will be heaven's verdict? Perhaps there will be a seminar on the Church of England? A case can be made today for leaving the Church of England but there is also a case for not deserting the sinking ship! Lee Gatiss clearly thinks there is a future for evangelicals in the Church of England, but admits that life will get increasingly difficult for them if they stay and fight:

> Those who dissent from the prevailing attitude of the powerful few at the heart of government on such issues, [as sexual morality] may yet find themselves in an unenviable position similar to that of the puritans of the Restoration era. Yet this should be interpreted not as a reason to despair but as an urgent call to continue reform of the denomination ... It would be foolish to abandon a leaky but serviceable vessel, and criminally negligent to find oneself thrown overboard merely for lack of proper attention to what was going on.[110]

I agree with that assessment. We should stay, and we should fight. I am encouraged by the significant number of young men who believe it right to do so. It seems that the question that was so important in 1662 is still with us today. Heaven in their eye didn't just help the Puritans to cope with their suffering but also to contend for the truth according to their reading of the Bible and their conscience. It can help us today.

What future for Bible churches in the UK?

I canvassed the views of a prominent non-conformist evangelical in Carlisle who shares many of my beliefs about the Bible to find out how he saw the future for Bible churches in the UK.

> Most of the issues we face at present are those faced by Christians everywhere—the assumption that to speak against homosexual practice or simply to affirm the Bible's teaching is to be assumed to be homophobic. The fact that we have those in our church who are homosexual by orientation and among our friends seems to be ignored! The biggest issue is faced by our people in the workplace, and when applying for funding for our social ministry—it is seemingly very difficult to obtain funding and be absolutely honest about our beliefs, and while some seem to be able to manage this we tend therefore to not apply for much outside funding and rely on our weekly offerings to sustain what is a growing financial burden. As yet Bedford jail seems a little way off as far as I am concerned, but many of our people in the health professions and care and social work, find themselves having to be increasingly careful about even mentioning their faith, let alone communicating what they believe in sensitive areas.

So Bedford jail is *a little way off* but the pressure on all Christians in the U.K. is increasing and we have a lot to learn from the Puritans about being prepared to suffer for the gospel.

In the next chapter we will examine how much heaven played a part in John Bunyan's classic *Pilgrim's Progress*. We will see how the term soldier-pilgrim applies to him and how he always kept heaven in his eye, no matter what he was discussing on earth.

10

Bunyan: Born for battle

Pilgrims Progress 1678

In this chapter we will seek to do three things: demonstrate that Bunyan was sustained in his struggles by his belief in heaven, make the point that the Christian is born for battle, and illustrate this by examining Bunyan's '*Pilgrim's Progress*'[III] which uses extended metaphors or *similitudes*. To illustrate the martial nature of Christianity I will develop an extended metaphor for this second section of the book based on my research into Hadrian's Wall. My family and I live in Carlisle not far from it.

Rome possessed the most successful army of antiquity. It conquered a massive empire and was built on the idea of recruiting and training professional legionnaires who served for twenty-five years under strict discipline, had no right to marry and would be given Roman citizenship and a plot of land for faithful service. Rome was not defeated ultimately from outside but from within, when conquered peoples with little commitment to Rome were needed to defend the vast empire, which had ceased growing. Instead of professional legionnaires with roots in Rome, many auxiliaries from conquered lands were used to defend the empire. The Emperor Hadrian began building a defensive wall right round the outer exposed parts of the empire as the period of expansion ceased, manned by these auxiliaries.

Part of these defences was Hadrian's Wall which lies between England and Scotland. Excavations since 1973 at a Roman fort at Vindolanda provide remarkable evidence to support this theory of inward collapse due to the employment of auxiliaries from conquered lands being used instead of professional soldiers from Rome. Military reports preserved on oak were discovered at Vindolanda in the local peat, which had deprived them of oxygen, thus delaying their decay. This unique find has given archaeologists rare evidence of what life in a Roman fort was like. What these reports reveal are details of mass desertions over a hundred years before the Barbarians entered Rome. These auxiliary legions lacked the commitment to the idea of Rome since they missed their own homeland and often married with local women and deserted to live in their villages. They were not true Romans but were conquered peoples who had other allegiances. Whilst defending Hadrian's Wall these troops faced three pressures: the pull of the local culture to marry and settle down, the attacks of warlike Picts and the intrigues of local chieftains. Several large finds of Roman gold given to local chieftains support the idea that the Roman peace was being bought from local warlords rather than won on the battlefield.

This is a similar situation to what the Christian faces as

he seeks to be faithful to his calling. We are tempted to be like those auxiliaries who were responsible for the Roman Empire collapsing from within. The Bible tells us that we face a trinity of evil: the world, the flesh and the devil. The world tries to mould us and convince us to give up the fight like the auxiliaries tempted to marry into the local culture and become assimilated. Lots of tiny shoes found at the Roman fort at Vindolanda show that many soldiers broke with the rule not to marry and have children. The flesh is the equivalent of the aggressive Pictish warriors who would constantly attack the auxiliaries and then melt away only to return the next day. The old nature never gives up the fight! We are to be constantly vigilant. The devil is represented in this analogy by the clever local chieftain who is the 'ringmaster' controlling and manipulating by threats and lies in order to intimidate the local defenders into some form of détente rather than taking up arms and being on a constant war footing.

John Bunyan in *Pilgrim's Progress* uses *similitudes* like these to describe the Christian as a soldier-pilgrim. He addresses each of the three powers that face the Christian soldier: he must endure Vanity Fair (in my analogy the world pictured by the local culture); he must daily fight his old sinful nature, (the implacable Pictish warrior harrying the auxiliary); and he must stand against Apollyon, (the local chieftain who manipulated the situation to get money from the Roman fort as the price of peace whilst at the same time stirring up trouble). Bunyan shows that the Christian must nerve himself for the fight and not expect the road to heaven to be a bed of roses. This is illustrated by the martyrdom of his godly companion Faithful.

In Chapter One of this book I referred to the idea that is quite widespread in the church today that becoming a Christian will make life easier. Bunyan teaches through *Pilgrim's Progress* that becoming a Christian will make life much harder, as we grapple with the evil within ourselves, with evil in the world and with the Evil One himself. Bunyan's classic will help us to be realistic about this battle and equip us with resources to *fight the good fight*. Bunyan experienced severe oppression and struggle in his own life, which resulted in his imprisonment in Bedford jail. What gave him the strength to carry on was his vision of heaven.

In this chapter I will use Bunyan's introductory remarks to *Pilgrim's Progress*, the outline of his book, to form the structure of my comments about how heaven was dominant in his thinking. He says that his book is,

> From This World to That Which is to Come; Delivered under the Similitude of a Dream. Wherein is discovered, the manner of his setting out, his dangerous journey; and safe arrival at the desired country.

1. From This World to That Which is to Come—
a twin view of heaven and earth

Pilgrim's Progress is a classic treatment of the generally-held Puritan view of the twin realities of heaven and earth, what I am calling in my book 'Heaven in your Eye and earth on your heart'. The Roman soldier was to be sustained for twenty-five years by his vision of 'heaven', a small parcel of land he could call home and the highly coveted right of citizenship within the Roman Empire. The Christian soldier is also sustained by *That Which is to Come*. The Christian is a soldier-pilgrim. He is travelling to a heavenly country and this world is not his home. He looks forward to his heavenly reward. Jesus promised that in his father's house there were many rooms. He went there to prepare a place for his followers.

In his autobiography Bunyan reveals one of his core values which is to live upon God that is invisible, the best way to go through sufferings, being

> to trust in God through Christ, as touching the world to come; and as touching this world, to count the grave my house, to make my bed in darkness.[112]

Like Calvin before him Bunyan counted this life on earth as a 'sepulchre'. This approach enabled him to die to this world and live for the next and even face persecution and imprisonment. The way of earthly renunciation is the way of heavenly peace. If you focus on heaven you will get earth thrown in: if you focus on earth you will get neither. By giving up all we gain all.

It is possible to overstate Bunyan's sufferings since he was allowed by some jailors to come and go at times from his prison cell and would have been released if he had been willing to agree not to preach. However, we also must not understate his sufferings and those of his family either. In *Grace Abounding* he describes the loss of a normal family life and the financial and emotional hardship it cost him and his loved ones:

> The parting with my Wife and poor Children hath oft been to me in this place as the pulling the flesh from my bones; and that not only because I am somewhat too fond of these great

mercies, but also because I should have often brought to my mind the many hardships, miseries, and wants that my poor family was like to meet with, should I be taken from them, especially my poor blind Child, who lay nearer my heart than all I had besides.[113]

However his core belief to live upon God that is invisible meant that he had to die to everything on earth including his own wants and his family's needs. This passion to only live for heaven came from his reading of the New Testament. In Colossians 3:2 Paul says, 'Set your minds on things that are above, not on things that are on earth'. Peter commands the Christian to 'set your hope fully on the grace that will be brought to you at the revelation of Jesus Christ' 1 Peter 1:13. Bunyan took these truths seriously and was willing to 'count everything as loss', as Paul writes in Philippians 3:8, 'that I may gain Christ'. In *Pilgrim's Progress* part one Christian warns his family of the wrath of God that is coming but when they refuse to listen he sets off towards the celestial city alone. Part two tells how his wife and children set off on the heavenly journey after him and find their sins forgiven and eternal rest for themselves.

Some would see Christian's sacrifice of himself and his family to seek the salvation of his own soul as an expression of individualism but this would be to misunderstand. The Puritans taught that sin has led to alienation from our Creator and Lord and when we find salvation, order is brought to both our private and public worlds. As the vertical relationship to God is put right it affects our horizontal relationship to our fellow man in radical ways. We become better husbands, wives, mothers, citizens and workers. In union with Christ we become part of his Church and we move from self and godlessness to God and selflessness. In a culture that has deified the individual and in which believers are tempted to be consumers rather than contenders, Bunyan's life focused on his Lord and upon heaven, is a great example to us. It was not that he was careless or thoughtless of his responsibilities it was that his commitment to the Lord came first. Bunyan was no hypocrite since he lived out the message of his books. In the words of another Puritan, Thomas Watson, 'he lived out his meditations'. Bunyan was willing to suffer the loss of all things, including his life, in order to be faithful to his heavenly calling. He was willing to *fight the good fight* on his way to heaven. Are we willing to do this today? This is very challenging for us.

2. The manner of his setting out—he runs

Pilgrim reads about the judgment that is coming and he decides to flee from the city of destruction. He pleads with his wife and family to flee but they think he is mad. He is so fearful and believing of the wrath of God that he runs continually during the first half of the book.

> Then said Evangelist, 'If this be thy condition, why standest thou still?' He answered, 'Because I know not whither to go.' Then he gave him a parchment roll, and there was written within, 'Fly from the wrath to come.' Matthew 3:7.

> The man therefore read it, and looking upon Evangelist very carefully, said, 'Whither must I fly?' Then said Evangelist, (pointing with his finger over a very wide field,) 'Do you see yonder wicket-gate?' Matthew 7:13, 14. The man said, 'No.' Then said the other, 'Do you see yonder shining light?' Psalm 119:105;

2 Peter 1:19. He said, 'I think I do.' Then said Evangelist, 'Keep
that light in your eye, and go up directly thereto, so shalt thou
see the gate; at which, when thou knockest, it shall be told thee
what thou shalt do.' So I saw in my dream that the man began
to run.

Why does he run? Bunyan recognizes the seriousness of sin
and God's judgment but I wonder if it also reflects the struggle
Bunyan had with himself and his personality. Dr Gaius Davies
argues that Bunyan had the classic symptoms of 'severe obsessive-
compulsive disorder'. Davies is not trying to reduce Bunyan's
spiritual experience to a mental disorder but to show that the
two strands, his spiritual suffering because he took the word of
God so seriously and his excessive anxiety were entwined. Bunyan
struggled to find peace with himself as well as peace with God.
Davies concludes, 'Both aspects were true and valid: Bunyan was
ill with his unhappiness, and also, spiritually he was moving from
darkness to light, from the City of Destruction to the Celestial
City'.[114] Davies says 'the struggles of Bunyan's own spiritual life
form the basis from which the content of *Pilgrim's Progress* is
drawn. Thus I think that the Slough of Despond, Giant Despair
and Doubting Castle are written out of his own experience of
depression … This may seem so obvious that it does not need
stating. It seems to me that Christians quite often believe it is
somehow a denial of their faith to be depressed. Bunyan would
not agree'.[115] This insight is of enormous benefit in terms of
mental and spiritual wellbeing. When a Christian goes through
the storms of life he is tempted to minimise the emotional toll
that suffering brings upon himself and his family. Bunyan's
experience lends hope that such a struggle, if it is based upon a
desire for peace with God, will eventually lead to being at peace

with oneself. Bunyan's struggles echoed in *Pilgrim's Progress* eventually led him to experience peace in his own personality after many years of struggle and trauma.

3. His dangerous journey—full of threats and enemies to fight

One potential drawback of Bunyan having a single main character 'Christian', involved in spiritual warfare, could be to give the impression that such warfare is conducted alone. There are other characters in *Pilgrim's Progress* like Evangelist and Faithful who fight alongside Christian but we could get the impression that Bunyan is suggesting we fight mainly alone. If I was to want to fight for Britain I would need to join the army like my brother Jim, be trained and equipped and then be sent out with others to fight. It is the same in the spiritual realm. Bunyan was a keen student of the Bible and he knew that before you get to Ephesians chapter six there are five other chapters! The warrior of chapter six is a corporate warrior. In chapter one there is the body; chapter two the new man, the house of God and the building; chapter three the church; the body and the new man in chapter four and the bride in chapter five. All these images are corporate not individual. So when we think about spiritual warfare pictured by Bunyan in *Pilgrim's Progress* we must think corporately. On this dangerous journey we are not alone and we fight together just as the Roman legionnaires famously linked shields to form a human tortoise for defence and attack. This is done by the local and worldwide church joining together in prayer for God's kingdom to advance.

On this journey we must adopt a fighting stance. You are a soldier-pilgrim like Christian in *Pilgrim's Progress*. You are in the Lord's army. The world, the flesh and Satan are against you. Expect opposition. In fact the Puritans believed that they would only make progress against opposition. When you meet severe opposition don't be put off but be encouraged that you are in the real battle for souls. The battle is hard and bloody. When the fight comes don't think it is a disaster but nerve yourself for the struggle. The Christian fights Apollyon in *Pilgrim's Progress* and he has to run the gauntlet of opposition in Vanity Fair and contend with his own sinful human nature. Christ is our captain; the cross is our banner and there will be much praying and weeping but 'Who suffers wins', unlike the SAS whose slogan is 'Who dares wins!' We need to be willing to suffer like Job and dare like Daniel.

There are three spiritual foes and I shall make brief comments on each regarding the warfare of the Christian.

a. *Pilgrim must endure Vanity Fair, the temptation to desertion and compromise.*

Just as the auxiliary needed to maintain his warlike posture and resist the pressure to settle down, so must the Christian. If he is a true believer then he is more akin to the spirit of the legionnaires from Rome. Because they belonged to Rome they were willing to lay down their lives if necessary. The auxiliary soldiers did not have that commitment and vision and they were very quickly assimilated bringing Rome's eventual collapse. These auxiliaries are akin to those who come to the church to meet personal needs rather than to live for Christ. Speaking to other ministers I find this to be a serious problem; as one non-conformist minister put it:

There are more 'believers' who have made decisions for Christ, but have not fully embraced a Biblical position on moral and lifestyle choices—discipleship is much harder among the pick'n'mix generations tainted by post-modernism.

I have found this in my own ministry. It seems like we have more in our churches with an 'auxiliary' mindset than a 'legionnaire' attitude. These folk need help to grow and mature. Perhaps this process is taking longer?

I have just read the biography of John Newton by Jonathan Aitken. In it he makes it clear how long it took for Newton's first stirrings of faith to fully mature. It is particularly striking how long Newton continued in the slave trade after he was first converted in a storm. This made me ponder my own long wanderings and struggles as a young Christian. What helped John Newton was finding pastors and mentors who would model maturity, since those we admire we seek to be like. This has been true for periods of growth in my life. The challenge then is to model and mentor others into maturity. When you read the story of John Bunyan the same pattern emerges of early wanderings and struggles until someone became a spiritual mentor and model. With support from such spiritually mature friends we have the confidence to enter the battle with sin, the world and the devil. We cease to be auxiliaries and become legionnaires. Christian has the help of Evangelist, Interpreter and a host of other spiritual friends along the journey and these friends equip him and support him in the battles ahead. We saw in chapter six how the Puritans believed the Church bound for heaven was at the heart of God's plans and Bunyan recognised the importance of being part of the Lord's army rather than operating as a lone ranger.

As a member of God's army Bunyan shows in *Pilgrim's Progress* that the Christian is to adopt the stance of continuous warfare and cannot drop his guard. He must be aware of the enemy and engage in the struggle with God's strength (Ephesians 6:10 'be strong in the Lord and in the strength of his might').

Vanity Fair was Bunyan's description of the world that is opposed to Christ and his Kingdom. Worldliness is rooted deeply within the modern church. Bunyan's work makes us aware of the dangers and helps provide the resources to change things for the better. Bunyan writes,

> Then I saw in my dream, that when they were got out of the wilderness, they presently saw a town before them, and the name of that town is Vanity; and at the town there is a fair kept, called Vanity Fair. It is kept all the year long. It beareth the name of Vanity Fair, because the town where it is kept is lighter than vanity, Psalm 62:9; and also because all that is there sold, or that cometh thither, is vanity; as is the saying of the wise, 'All that cometh is vanity.' ... Here are to be seen, too, and that for nothing, thefts, murders, adulteries, false-swearers, and that of a blood-red colour.

The Pilgrims have arrived in a place identical to the one they have already fled from, the city of destruction. Philip Edwards resolves this problem for us when he writes,

The journey takes him [Christian] to Vanity Fair, which is of course the very City of Destruction which he had left long before. It is a different city because Christian has become a different man. That city which he had once dwelt contentedly in, then fled from in fear, he now enters as a convinced Christian, ready to put up with whatever mockery, abuse, and violence may be directed at him. Faithful and Christian are no longer citizens of the City of Destruction; they are pilgrims and strangers in it.[116]

Bunyan's *Pilgrim's Progress* is from a personal to a public wilderness, the wilderness of the world as the Reformers called it. We too must live in this place until we go to be with the Lord in heaven. However we are to be in the world but not of it.

b. *Pilgrim must daily fight his old sinful nature: his implacable enemy, the Pictish warrior.*

Paul warns us in Romans 8:13, 'For if you live according to the flesh you will die, but if by the Spirit you put to death the deeds of the body, you will live'.

The flesh will seek to get us to take *Bye-path Meadow*. Christian and his friend come to a very difficult part of the path but then find just over a stile a lush meadow running parallel that is much easier. I am sure they only planned to be there for a short period of rest before rejoining the main path, but the paths gradually part and night falls and they soon find themselves in a place of gloom and despair.

The flesh tells us that we don't have to take the difficult and narrow path but that we should take the easier broad road. We don't need to go to the celestial city via the cross. We can have our reward here on earth and on the other side too since God is love. We can have a crown without battling against the flesh. Bunyan shows the danger of Bye-path Meadow thinking and has his hero quickly rejoin the path that leads to suffering and then to life. He knows from the Apostle that 'through many tribulations we must enter the kingdom of God' (Acts 14:22). He knows that the crown is not given to the one who calls Jesus Saviour but the one who finishes the race and wins the prize (2 Timothy 2:5).

Bunyan teaches us that this implacable foe, the enemy within, never sleeps and we must be constantly vigilant and resist its influence. Paul tells us that we need to constantly *put to death the misdeeds of the body* if we are to have life. In chapter thirteen we will discuss the need for self-control and discipline in Bunyan's *The Heavenly Runner*, which shares some of the ideas of *Pilgrim's Progress*.

c. *Pilgrim must stand against Apollyon.*

The local chieftain near Hadrian's Wall manipulated the situation to get money and influence. Apollyon is the 'ringmaster' in Bunyan's story. Who is Apollyon? In Revelation 9:11 we read of him:

> They have as king over them the angel of the bottomless pit. His name in Hebrew is Abaddon, and in Greek he is called Apollyon.

Apollyon is another word for the devil. The fact that Apollyon is a King suggests he is the devil or one of his senior officers. Bunyan's Apollyon is a symbolic representation of our spiritual enemy but he is inspired by a real being who opposes God's people, the 'accuser of the brethren' (Revelation 12:10), who one day will be thrown into the 'lake of burning sulphur' (Revelation 20:10).

Bunyan describes the meeting of Christian and Apollyon in the following way:

> So he went on, and Apollyon met him. Now the monster was hideous to behold: he was clothed with scales like a fish, and they are his pride; he had wings like a dragon, and feet like a bear, and out of his belly came fire and smoke; and his mouth was as the mouth of a lion. When he was come up to Christian, he beheld him with a disdainful countenance, and thus began to question him.

> APOLLYON: Whence came you, and whither are you bound?

> CHRISTIAN: I am come from the city of Destruction, which is the place of all evil, and I am going to the city of Zion.

> APOLLYON: By this I perceive thou art one of my subjects; for all that country is mine, and I am the prince and god of it. How is it, then, that thou hast run away from thy king? Were it not that I hope thou mayest do me more service, I would strike thee now at one blow to the ground.

This is Bunyan at his most imaginative and speculative but

he is careful to remain rooted in the biblical revelation of the enemy of souls. His portrayal shows how monstrous the devil is when not hidden as an angel of light (2 Corinthians 11:14). He is hideous to behold. Clearly Christian feels intimidated by the monster but this passage shows Christian's resolution to continue to the City of Zion.

In the battle scene with Apollyon we are shown the need for active faith in opposing evil. First when faced by the prospect of doing battle Christian is tempted to turn his back and withdraw but remembers he has no armour on his back and therefore determines to stand fast. The devil seeks to frighten him with tales of those who belong to 'this other prince [Jesus] whose lives have been lost in his cause'. Christian replies that such things are the test to see whether they will remain totally faithful to him to the end. Christian says he is travelling on the King's highway, the way of holiness. We saw in chapter five how holiness to the Lord was a key Puritan concept. When Apollyon attacks Christian resists manfully using both the shield of faith and the sword of the Spirit, the word of God. This battle goes on for half a day until Christian is almost vanquished and lies fallen at Apollyon's feet about to be killed, when picking up his fallen sword Christian strikes his enemy with words from Romans chapter eight, declaring that we are more than conquerors through him who loved us. At this Apollyon leaves him for a season with Christian exhausted but undefeated. It is significant that Christian's quotation refers to believers in the plural, again pointing to the fact that spiritual warfare must be done together rather than alone. This incident shows the reality of spiritual struggle and the need to face opposition with faith in God and in the word of God rather than to turn tail and run. It echoes the way our Prince, the Lord Jesus, defeated the devil in his forty day temptation in the wilderness by appealing to the word of God.

4. His safe arrival at the desired country

Having passed over safely the river of death Christian and Hopeful enter heaven. We will look at the issue of death in the final chapter of the book but here let us focus on the joyful arrival of God's people into the celestial city as described by Bunyan in *Pilgrim's Progress*:

> Now upon the bank of the river, on the other side, they saw the two shining men again who there waited for them; wherefore, being come up out of the river, they saluted them, saying, 'We are ministering spirits, sent forth to minister for those that shall be heirs of salvation.' Thus they went along towards the gate. Now you must note that the City stood upon a mighty hill; but the pilgrims went up that hill with ease, because they had these two men to lead them up by the arms; also they had left their mortal garments behind them in the river; for though they went in with them, they came out without them. They therefore went up here with much agility and speed; though the foundation upon which the City was framed was higher than the clouds. They therefore went up through the regions of the air, sweetly talking as they went; being comforted, because they safely got over the river, and had such glorious companions to attend them.

Christian and Hopeful are welcomed and escorted by two angels and helped up the mighty hill where the celestial city stood. Then they are greeted by the citizens of Heaven with trumpet blasts and great shouts of joy. Just before they reached the gate they were told by the two angels who told them that the beauty and glory of it was inexpressible. They would meet

> an innumerable company of angels; they would see the tree of life, and eat of the never-fading fruit ... you shall have white robes given you, and best of all, your walk and talk shall be every day with the King, even all the days of eternity.[117]

As they arrived at the gate they gave in their certificates which were carried to the King, who then commanded for the gates to be opened and as they entered they were transfigured, their rags fell off and they had clothes that

> shone like gold ... Then I heard in my dream, that all the bells in the city rang again for joy, and that it was said unto them, 'Enter ye into the joy of our Lord'.[118]

Their battles are over and their joy begins! They have gone home to be with God.

However, as Jesus said, 'in this world you will have tribulation' (John 16:33). In the next chapter we will see how Richard Baxter, a prominent Episcopal Puritan, battled against false teaching and fought for Christian unity because he had 'heaven in his eye and earth on his heart'.

11

Baxter: fighting the wolves and loving the lambs for heaven

The Reformed Pastor 1656

When I was a School's Worker in the 1980s employed by a trust connected to Capernwray Bible School near Lancaster I was a member of a local Anglican church but was invited to preach around the non-conformist churches in the area. The conversation after the service at these churches over coffee would follow a familiar pattern. They would say: 'We really enjoyed what you had to share with us from the Bible, but we are perplexed that you can still belong to something like the Anglican Church'. When this happened I would walk over with them to their bookstall and point out how many books on it were written by Anglican evangelicals like John Stott, Jim Packer and Dick Lucas! Sadly such prejudice still exists within some non-conformist circles but hopefully things are changing for the better. Unity and mutual respect between believers in our Lord Jesus is something he prayed for in John 17.

Richard Baxter was an Anglican Puritan who became a reluctant non-conformist but he has much to teach us about fighting the wolves and loving the lambs for heaven. Baxter had a 'legionnaire' attitude to his calling rather than the commonly held 'auxiliary' attitude of détente of many Christians today in the UK. He was prepared to fight false teaching. He exercised zero tolerance. However, when it came to orthodox believers he showed a remarkable willingness to unite on the gospel. 'Richard Baxter preached theological unity during a century of schism, and advocated mutual respect within the church during a period of intense religious warfare'.[119] I want to advance the thesis contained in the quotation above, *that Baxter preached theological unity during an age of schism*; and that he was energized in part by his vision of heaven. Dallas Willard suggested that instead of trying to get as many people into heaven conservative Christians should try to get heaven into people! Baxter wants to do both and so do I! Greater unity amongst true believers would bring more of heaven down to earth. Getting heaven into people is not about fuzzy feelings but fighting the wolves and loving the lambs for heaven. Having the priority of heaven and the realities of eternity made Baxter passionate to save souls and also to protect them from harm and build them up in their faith so they would be ready for heaven. Getting heaven into believers will make us more willing to fight the wolves. I believe we need to get people into heaven *and* heaven into people. In this chapter the focus will be more on the latter but both are vital for the growth and health of God's church.

In this chapter we will look at *The Reformed Pastor*, a book that is still very popular with ministers today and was written for a gathering of ministers Baxter was due to preach to but was unable because of illness. Instead of attending he sent them his sermon notes instead! The subject of his notes was that ministry should have two aims:

> The ultimate end of our pastoral oversight must be linked with the ultimate purpose of our whole lives. This is to please and glorify God. It is also to see the sanctification and holy obedience of the people under our charge.[120]

The glory of God and the blessing of the people in the parish were Baxter's twin aims and they should be ours today. This reflects heaven in your eye (God's glory) and earth in your heart (God's blessing on people). As with the tension between heaven and earth, we will see a tension between seeking unity and defending the Church against error. Baxter was a controversialist but he had a great passion for the unity of true Christians and was disturbed by tendencies for secondary issues to separate those who should be working together in the gospel. John Bunyan believed in believer's baptism but recognised this as a secondary issue. Uniting around the fundamentals of the gospel was something the best Puritans were able to do and it is something we need to aim for today. Baxter will help us to see who our gospel friends should be and who our enemies are so that we can embrace the one and fight the other, just as the good shepherd loves the sheep and drives off the wolves. These practical concerns reflect the spiritual awareness the Puritans had of heaven and hell.

1. Fighting the wolves

Baxter sees Christian leadership in the context of a battle against spiritual forces.[121]

> You have undertaken to be under Christ, to lead a band of His soldiers against principalities and powers and spiritual wickedness in high places. You must, then, lead them through the sharpest battles. You must learn the enemy's strategy and battle plans. You must watch yourself and keep your hand vigilant. For if you fail, they and you, too, may perish. You have a subtle enemy, so you must be wise. You have a vigilant enemy and so you must be watchful. You have a malicious, violent, and unwearied enemy, so you must be resolute, courageous, and unwearied. You are in a crowd of enemies, encompassed by them on every side; and if you heed one and not all, you will quickly fall. So what a task you have before you!

Being an under-shepherd of Christ is an awesome calling, which involves spiritual warfare and the recognition of a heaven to be won or lost. Baxter pictures the Christian's conflict in martial terms, pointing to the need for both vigilance and wisdom. These ideas came from the New Testament. We must not underestimate our enemy for he is like a roaring lion looking for someone to devour (1 Peter 5:8–9). He can transform himself into an angel of light (2 Corinthians 11:14). If we think we can stand in our own strength we will quickly be overwhelmed (1 Corinthians 10:12). The Bible says that the Spirit led Jesus into the wilderness to be tempted, it was not his idea to take on the devil. (Matthew 4:1). Even the Son of God didn't venture out on his own but relied upon his heavenly Father (John 5:19). We must rely on the Father through the

Holy Spirit, as we put on our Christian armour, each piece put on with prayer (Ephesians 6:10–18). As we seek to be faithful to our commanding officer, the captain of the Lord of Hosts (Joshua 5:14), we need, says Baxter, to keep our eyes on the goal of heaven, where a 'crown of righteousness' awaits us. We are to

So gird up the loins of your minds, and conduct yourselves like men, that you may end your days with Paul's triumphant confidence. 'I have fought the good fight. I have kept the faith. I have finished my course. Henceforth, is laid up for me a crown of righteousness, which God the righteous Judge, shall give me' (2 Timothy 4:7).[122]

Knowing *the enemy's strategy and battle plans* will make us realistic about the fight. As well as the commonly understood: 'divide and conquer' approach, the enemy of souls regularly employs the strategy of attacking the shepherd to destroy the sheep:

Take heed to yourselves because the tempter will make his first and sharpest assault on you. If you will be leaders against him, he will not spare you. He bears the greatest malice against the man who is engaged in working the greatest damage against him. He hated Christ more than any of us, because He is the 'Captain of our Salvation'. So Satan hates the leaders under him more than ordinary soldiers. He knows full well what a rout he can cause among the followers if the leaders fall before their eyes. He smites the shepherd to scatter the flock.[123]

The enemy within the visible church

Baxter poses the question: How can you fight against Satan if you are one of his servants?

> It is disastrous that so many preachers of the Gospel have been enemies of the work of the Gospel which they preach. How many such traitors have been in the Church of Christ all ages! They have done more against Him under his colours than they could ever have done in the open field of battle against Him ... So many wolves have been set over the sheep, disguised in sheep's clothing! Pretending to be a Christian they are not. If there were a traitor among the twelve in Christ's family, it is no marvel that there be many such today.[124]

Baxter speaks both positively and negatively of bishops:

> If only would-be leaders in the church might be contented with the sufficient word of God, and not impose new canons and authorities over it. Then I would not disobey such a bishop.[125]

> Yet, thank God, not all the prelates of the Church miscarried justice ... such leaders as Bishop James Ussher and Joseph Hall, learned, godly, and peaceable men. But they, too, were maligned for their purity and soundness of faith, and they, too, were scorned as Puritans.[126]

I am fortunate that my present Bishop in Carlisle is a godly man. After an excellent study at the Cathedral on Jesus' teaching on the Sermon on the Mount, I asked him in the question time about Matthew 7:15–16, where Jesus warns his disciples,

> Beware of false prophets, who come to you in sheep's clothing but inwardly are ravenous wolves. You will recognize them by their fruits. Are grapes gathered from thornbushes, or figs from thistles?

My question was: 'Are there false teachers in the House of Bishops?'

His reply was tactful but helpful. He said, 'There are two ways of looking at Scripture in the House of Bishops that cannot be reconciled'.

The Church of England is like a house divided against itself

This unbridgeable chasm within the Church of England was shown very clearly by *The Pilling Report* published in November 2013. The working party chaired by Sir Joseph Pilling, a retired civil service mandarin, was asked to report on human sexuality for the House of Bishops. Whilst there are admirable recommendations to combat homophobia, the Report, advocates same sex blessings by the back door. One member of the group was Keith Sinclair, the Bishop of Birkenhead, who authored a 'dissenting report', which is a devastating critique on how the Report lacks a proper theological and biblical underpinning to its main recommendation, which is to move away from the Church of England's present official position of regarding homosexual practice as falling short of God's plan for human sexuality, and to allow same-sex blessings. Strong action needs to be taken by bishops and Anglican evangelical and charismatic churches and networks to distance orthodox believers from this liberal break with the clear teaching of the Bible. These issues, as we have said already, are affecting all the churches in England. It is not just an Anglican problem.

There is no discipline in the church

Discipline was one of the marks of the true church developed in the Reformation. Baxter laments that 'there is scarcely such a thing as church discipline in all the land'. No one is rebuked publicly for open sin and no one excommunicated 'for the vilest of offences'. On the other hand the persecution of the Puritans had gathered pace and 'many thousands of godly pastors and their families left England to go to the continent of Europe, and most of all to America'. Because of the general public attitude of the times, 'any man who protested against the lawlessness of the Church would immediately be jeered at as a Puritan'.[127]

There is an unbridgeable gulf within the Anglican Communion and the Church of England between the orthodox and those with a revisionist agenda who reject the authority of Scripture. This is reflected within other denominations like the Baptist Union and the Methodist Church. This was what the Bishop of Carlisle was alluding to in his answer to my question in the Cathedral when he spoke of 'two ways of looking at Scripture in the House of Bishops that cannot be reconciled'. As Jesus said: A house divided against itself cannot stand.

Choose carefully who you read and who you listen to

Baxter advises care in what you allow into your mind!

> In your reading, will you not choose authors who speak the truth plainly—even bluntly so—rather than those who speak eloquently but falsely.[128]

I tell my flock to read Christian books by authors who stick to the Scriptures as they have been faithfully interpreted by the teachers and doctors of the church through the ages. I also warn them to listen carefully to sermons, especially those of their vicar! The noble Bereans even checked out what Paul the Apostle was saying by comparing it with the Old Testament Scriptures (Acts 17:11). A good test of books and preachers is to ask not just what they affirm but what they refuse to condemn. The Bible is both culture positive and culture negative. The Church of England does not exist to be a Chaplain to the nation but to be its prophet and evangelist! It is not whether a preacher is entertaining or a nice man but whether he is basing his message faithfully in the Scriptures or simply applying it from his own worldly thinking. Lay folk should look for faithful Bible-teaching churches whether Anglican or non-conformist. On holiday my wife and I find a Bible teaching church to worship in irrespective of whether it is Anglican or non-conformist.

2. Loving the sheep for heaven

Get heaven right and everything else will fit into place
Baxter would heartily agree with the statement quoted from C. S. Lewis on Christian hope in the first chapter of the book that if we get heaven right we will get 'earth thrown in'; but if we get heaven wrong we will get neither. Like Boston, Baxter

shows the essential nature of the new birth to make people holy
for heaven:

> The misery of the unconverted is so great that it calls for
> our utmost compassion. They are in the grip of bitterness ...
> They have no part in the pardon of their sins nor in the hope of
> glory. We are therefore driven by necessity to 'open their eyes,
> and to turn them from darkness to light, and from the power
> of Satan unto God: that they may receive forgiveness of sins,
> and inheritance among the sanctified by faith in Christ' (Acts
> 26:18).[129]

Again like Boston, Baxter extols the beauty and perfections of
heaven to build believers up in their faith.

Baxter says that,

> By showing men the certainty and the excellence of the
> promised joy, and by making them aware of the perfect
> blessedness of the life to come in comparison with the vanities
> of the present life, we may redirect their understanding and
> affections towards heaven. We shall bring them to the point
> of due contempt of this world and fasten their hearts on a
> more durable treasure. This is the work we should be busy
> with both night and day. For when we have affixed their hearts
> unfeignedly on God and heaven, the major part of our ministry
> is accomplished. All the rest will follow naturally.[130]

Fixing hearts on heaven, says Baxter, is a major part of our
work, yet how much time do we give to it in the church today?

This will involve both saving souls for heaven and bringing heaven into souls.

Fight for unity based on grace, truth and wisdom

'There is a great need', Baxter concludes, 'to settle our own quarrels [within the Puritans], to be tolerant unto godly men who have retained Episcopal offices and not give up hope for the future ministry within the church'. There are today in the house of Bishops, as in Baxter's day, 'learned, godly, and peaceable men'.[131]

We must seek to encourage bishops who are orthodox and work with everyone we can in the service of the gospel. It is a scandal of evangelicalism that we find it so difficult to work with other evangelicals who love the Lord, perhaps more passionately than we do, but differ on some secondary issues. Baxter calls for humility, 'to heal the schisms and differences of conviction among all true pastors of the church'. He says peace and harmony could be arrived at, 'if we sought to love one another unfeignedly and seek unity earnestly' but too often, 'we read and preach on those texts that command men to follow peace with all men and to live peaceably with them, and yet we are so far from its practice that we snarl at, malign, and censure one another'.[132]

When the Archbishop of Sydney, Peter Jensen made a preaching tour of England in 2003 he lamented that evangelical ministry in the UK had been held back by personality problems between leaders. There was some repentance over that and his challenge helped start a number of gospel partnerships across the denominations and in various part of the country. This is good and must be continued. Baxter says,

> Ministers have need of one another. They need to improve the gifts of God in each other. For the self-sufficient are the most deficient. He is unfitted to be a pastor unless he delights in holiness, hates iniquity, loves the unity and purity of the Church, and abhors discord and division.[133]

Baxter is talking about unity based upon truth. This unity amongst orthodox Bible-believing Christians must have a greater priority. The recent GAFCON conference in Nairobi that I was privileged to attend was a good example of the sort of unity in diversity we need to develop amongst Bible-believing Christians. As well as thirty-eight nations represented amongst the fourteen hundred delegates there was a wide diversity of outward style. The Sydney Anglicans led by Peter Jensen usually wear shirts and ties rather than dog collars whilst the largest delegation of Nigerian Anglicans are part of a high-church tradition and normally wear copes and mitres (the bishops that is!). During the conference both groups sought to make accommodation to each other: the Sydney Anglicans wore dog collars and the Nigerians left their copes and mitres at home! Whilst these may seem small concessions they signified a real desire to unite around the truth of the gospel.

Storms ahead for conservative evangelicals

One of our problems as conservative evangelical Anglicans is that we have no one in the present House of Bishops who represents our theological position since all bishops support women becoming vicars and bishops. The Reform Covenant supports

> The unique value of women's ministry in the local congregation but also the divine order of male headship, which makes the headship of women as priests in charge, incumbents, dignitaries and bishops inappropriate.

In Baxter's day there were a few Puritan bishops who shared their position they could turn to. We need bishops like them! We urgently need representation in the House of Bishops. A recent Church of England report highlighted this but nothing has been done. It is difficult to avoid the conclusion that whilst we are told that we are recognised as 'legitimately Anglican', we are tolerated rather than valued in the present Church of England. In this regard we are like the Puritans in 1662.

Another problem is that whilst liberal bishops seem to have the confidence to speak publicly on doctrinal matters, orthodox bishops tend to be silent. Whether the combination of the Global Anglican Future movement on one hand and *The Pilling Report* on the other will galvanise the orthodox bishops in the House of Bishops into concerted and united action in defence of key Christian doctrine remains to be seen. I hope they will find their courage but it will be costly in the current cultural climate.

Today in the UK anyone who attempts to speak against the tide of immorality sweeping our nation is likely to face the same fate as several Christian street preachers arrested in the last few months for sharing what the Bible says on sexual ethics and other important issues. These are signs that whilst Bedford jail (where Bunyan was incarcerated for preaching without a licence) is still far in the distance for many, some have already had a taste of it! Fortunately all these preachers were released without charge but a clear pattern of the harassment of street preachers is undeniable. The days of Boston, Bunyan and Baxter are long gone but they still have much to teach us. They teach us that we need to fight the wolves and love the lambs for heaven and be ready for more opposition. Such willingness comes from a vision of heaven that makes us more like the 'legionnaire' of Rome than the 'auxiliary' serving on Hadrian's Wall. Such a vision will involve both saving souls for heaven and bringing heaven into souls. In chapter 12 we will see how important unity and mutual respect is for evangelicals as we look at the dilemma of his life faced by William Gurnall.

12

William Gurnall: Unsung hero

The Christian in Complete Armour 1665

Sir Winston Churchill was voted the greatest Briton of all time. Churchill was a great 'war leader', especially in the crisis that faced Britain in May 1940. But was he the greatest Briton? The greatest Briton that we know about, perhaps! The same could be said in answer to the question of who is the greatest Christian believer. Eternity's perspective may well be very different from earth's assessment. There must be many untold stories of great heroism that were never able to be told because the facts remained hidden or have been lost. Such is the story of William Gurnall, unsung hero of 1662. He is unsung because unlike many lesser Puritan writers, there is so little we know about him. Bishop J. C. Ryle takes the few fragments of what is known and pieces together a credible explanation of Gurnall's behaviour during the crisis of 1662. His explanations make sense, but are at best conjecture, since we know nothing of Gurnall's motives in accepting what two thousand godly fellow Puritans could not, the Act of Uniformity. However, there is some evidence that Ryle does not bring to the court of human opinion and that is Gurnall's book *The Christian in Complete Armour*, which has become a Puritan classic. This collection of his writings formed into one book tells us that he was a godly man and certainly no hypocrite. His vision of heaven in his eye and earth on his heart kept Gurnall true to his convictions to be a conforming Puritan. He is no 'auxiliary' serving on Hadrian's Wall but a 'legionnaire' of Rome!

When my brother Jim was in the army, I was a student teacher in Liverpool sharing a flat on Dragon Lane near Whiston Hospital with two other Christians, one of whom happened to be called John Owen. Two striking things happened whilst I was in the flat for a year. The first was that my future wife Gloria, who was training as a nurse at the nearby hospital, used to walk past my flat regularly and we never met! The second significant thing was just as surprising. So I could get to college, Jim reluctantly agreed to lend me his prized bicycle, a racer with eighteen gears! At Christmas the flat was empty as all three students were at home visiting family. When we returned to our flat in the New Year it had been burgled and my brother's bike was gone! I think he has forgiven me, but he's not forgotten! I'm sure he wouldn't trust me with his latest prize possession; a rather expensive sports car. My brother is not alone in his enjoyment of material things. All of us tend to get attached to possessions, but they are transient. As I looked adoringly at my brother's new red sports car I thought to myself, 'It will be a heap of rust in twenty years!' That thought made me feel so much better! William Gurnall, applying the warning of Jesus in Matthew 6:19–21, also has a healthy outlook that says that what we value should be looked at from the perspective of heaven rather than earth:

> Value yourselves by your inheritance in the other world, and not by your honour and riches in this.[134]

This comment sets the tone for Gurnall's book but also for the critical decisions he made in his life. Perhaps the most significant was what to do about the Act of Uniformity. Gurnall's choice to stay in the Church of England would not have pleased either his friends or his enemies, who would have all wanted him to leave for different reasons. His friends would want him to join them in making a big gesture and his enemies would want to get him out of the Church of England. In such 'hurricane' situations as 1662 a man's faith and hope are severely tested. The critical question asked of anyone in such circumstances would be: 'Is your hope founded in this life or in the life to come?' If we focus on heaven we get earth thrown in; if we choose to focus mainly on earth we get neither. Where did Gurnall's heart lie? If we want to find out what Gurnall said he believed then all we have to do is read his book. According to his writings his vision was certainly fixed on heaven. We have no reason to think he was a hypocrite. His focus on heaven, I believe, gave him the strength to follow the dictates of his conscience and stay in the Church of England. For Gurnall this was the right thing to do, whilst for others it was right for them to leave.

It is clear from a cursory reading of Gurnall's work *The Christian in Complete Armour*, that he is immersed in the

Puritan idea of the daily swaying battle with the world, the flesh and the devil; and the priority of looking to our heavenly home whilst caring for the earth as well. His writing is intensely practical. It is doctrine for life. In his introduction he writes of the Apostle Paul that,

> ... this holy man was not so fond of liberty or life, as to purchase them at the least hazard to the gospel. He knew too much of another world, to bid so high for the enjoying of this; and therefore he is regardless what his enemies can do to him, well knowing he should go to heaven whether they would or no.

Then Gurnall declares that 'the Christians calling is a continued warfare with the world, and the prince of the world'. In the first part of his argument he recounts the difficulties of Christian warfare, which means there are few who are 'fit for this calling'. There will be great struggles and 'the Christian's whole course of walking with God or acting for God is lined with many difficulties, which shoot like enemies through the hedges at him, while he is marching towards heaven'. Continuing this military metaphor of a non-stop battle with evil, Gurnall encourages Christians 'to labour for this holy resolution and prowess, which is so needful for your Christian profession, that without it you cannot be what you profess. The fearful are in the forlorn of those who march for hell, the violent and valiant are they which take heaven by force: cowards never won heaven'.

In the second part of his argument for taking on the whole armour of God his account is peppered with references to heaven: 'take heaven by storm and force', 'rallyings of their faith and patience got upon the walls of heaven', and 'crowned with heaven's glory'. He concludes with a powerful image of God and heaven watching this battle with evil and shouting encouragement to Christian fidelity and courage:

> In a word, Christians, God and angels are spectators, observing how you quit yourselves like children of the Most High; every exploit your faith doth against sin and Satan causeth a shout in heaven.

Gurnall pictures God and the angels as spectators of the swaying battle against sin the world and the devil, applauding and encouraging God's children as they 'fight the good fight of faith' and as they trample Satan under their feet.

This develops the idea of Jesus that 'there is joy before the angels of God over one sinner who repents' (Luke 15:10). If there is such joy in heaven over sinners beginning the walk of faith then it is logical that saints battling faithfully would raise a shout! John says something like that in 3 John 3: 'I rejoiced greatly when the brothers came and testified to your truth, as indeed you are walking in the truth'.

It is hard to believe that God finds such joy in his regenerate children but the Bible has many passages that say this. One of the most remarkable is Zephaniah 3:17

> The Lord your God is in your midst, a mighty one who will save; he will rejoice over you with gladness; he will quiet you by his love; he will exult over you with loud singing.

It's hard for us to believe that God sings over us as a bridegroom over his bride—but he does. We tend to feel so bad about ourselves that we think God must feel let down and very disappointed but he loves us as our Heavenly Father. Gurnall rightly points to the joy there is in heaven when we make any spiritual progress, but because we are in union with Christ, God the Father always looks lovingly upon us. Even when he is disciplining us we can be sure of his unfailing love for us (Hebrews 12:12). Puritans like Boston and Gurnall had heaven in their eye because of their union with Christ, which made them holy for heaven.

What about earth on your heart?

Whilst heaven is clearly the priority, earth is not forgotten or neglected by this godly man. Ryle writes in his introduction to Gurnall's book,

> He had a bountiful hand and plentiful purse (his paternal inheritance by death of elder brothers and other transactions, descending upon him), bequeathing twenty pounds in money, and ten pounds per annum, to the poor of the parish;[135]

According to Wikipedia £100 in Restoration times is about £5,600 in today's money. Gurnall's giving of ten pounds per year to the poor was indeed a generous act in giving about £560 a year in today's currency.

Having looked at the evidence of Gurnall's testimony from his own writing, we can now take evidence from those who through history have pondered his decision against the tide of two thousand fellow Puritans, to remain in his parish and conform to the Act of Uniformity. Did this decision undermine Gurnall's clear commitment to putting heaven rather than earth first, expressed so clearly in his book *The Christian in Complete Armour*? Was his decision to conform a mistake and indeed a sign of cowardice in the face of the enemy? I will now call my first witness, Bishop J. C. Ryle, who draws on the testimony of other notable evangelicals such as Spurgeon and Newton to make his case.

Bishop J. C. Ryle's introduction

Ryle provides us with just about all the information that can be gathered on William Gurnall in his introduction to *The Christian In Complete Armour*. It is striking that so little is known about the writer of such a well-known and well-loved Puritan book. Spurgeon thought Gurnall's book, 'Peerless and priceless; every line is full of wisdom; every sentence is suggestive ... The best thought-breeder *in all our library* (my italics).' John Newton was equally impressed, making the comment that, 'If I might read only one book beside the Bible, I would choose *The Christian in Complete Armour*. And yet we know almost nothing about the life of William Gurnall. Why is that? It seems likely that in situations where opinion is polarised as it was in the religious climate of 1662, no one likes a man who refuses to side with one of the opposing positions and instead follows a middle course. This is what William Gurnall chose to do and it is most likely that as a result he was not popular with either of the opposing sides; this goes a long way to explaining the lack of recorded information about him.

We cannot be sure of what motivated Gurnall to take this unusual step, but could it have been that he was more interested

in the souls of his flock than in taking sides in a political fight
to the death? This is not to question the motives of the majority
of godly Puritans who felt they could not sign the Act of
Uniformity and left the Church of England in 1662, but it does
open up a fascinating glimpse into the possibility that not all
the moral high ground integrity and courage lie with those who
make costly public decisions out of conscience. Perhaps it took
as much courage for Gurnall to remain at his post as it did for
those who felt they had to leave their parishes. This is certainly
what Ryle tentatively suggests may have been the case. As he
says,

> I leave the subject of Gurnall's conduct in 1662 with the
> reader. It is one on which different men will have different
> opinions, according to the standpoint which they occupy. Some
> in the present day would have thought more highly of Gurnall
> if he had refused to submit to the Act of Uniformity, and had
> gone out with the famous two thousand. I, and many others
> perhaps, think more highly of him because he held his ground
> and did not secede.[136]

We know that Gurnall was attacked from the Puritan side for
his acceptance of the Act of Uniformity. A libellous tract was
published in 1665, quoted by Bishop Kennett, which contains
the following passage:

> Neither is Mr. Gurnall alone in these horrible defilements,
> hateful to the word of God and his saints, but is compassed
> about with a cloud of witnesses, even in the same county
> where himself liveth, men of the same order of anti-Christian
> priesthood and brethren in the same iniquity with himself.

Ryle also tells us that Gurnall's father-in-law was one of the
two thousand godly Puritans who were ejected in 1662. One
can only imagine how much more difficult it was for him not to
follow the exodus if his own relative was directly involved. Did
this cause family tensions? It would not be surprising if it had
caused some difficulties on both sides. And then what about
feeding his large family? These are not easy matters to resolve
when your own flesh and blood are involved. John Bunyan
felt the pressures of remaining in Bedford jail when he had a
family to support that included a blind daughter. Ryle outlines
Gurnall's unfortunate circumstances when he writes,

> His own wife's father, Mr. Mott, of Stoke by Nayland,
> was one of the two thousand who went out of the Church of
> England for conscience' sake. Above all, the value of his living
> at Lavenham, and the large size of the family dependent on him,
> would be sure to cause men to cast suspicion on what he did,
> and to question the sincerity of his motives.

Ryle's interpretation of events

As Ryle admits, the facts regarding Gurnall's behaviour in 1662
are open to being interpreted in different ways. Gary Brady, for
example, writes of the importance of conscience of those who
did the right thing by leaving the Church of England in 1662,

> The Bible speaks about conscience often enough but it is a
> rather neglected subject among evangelicals today. The 1662
> men were men who knew they had a conscience and who were
> willing to act upon it with courage when necessary.[137]

This was certainly true for the two thousand godly Puritans

who in good conscience felt unable to accept the Act of Uniformity, but was it as simple as it sounds for every godly Puritan? Was another response possible that was equally brave that was also the result of keeping a clear conscience before the Lord?

Bishop J. C. Ryle provides this alternative perspective on how Gurnall acted in 1662, by stating that, 'I shall clear the way by saying that I thoroughly disapprove the Act of Uniformity, although personally I feel no difficulty about its requirements'. Whilst Ryle considered the Act of Uniformity 'unjust, impolitic, unstatesmanlike and a hard measure', he quite understood why Gurnall had acted as he did and Ryle thought that many good men could have thought the same about the situation. They would have argued that we cannot expect everything the way we want in life; that patience is a virtue rather than secession; that there is nothing wrong in using set forms of prayer as such; that it is better to accept the Prayer Book with its imperfections rather than lose precious opportunities for the gospel so long as the Thirty-Nine Articles were retained and they were not forced to preach unsound doctrine. They should not refuse to preach and look after the flocks entrusted to their care. All these thoughts a good man like Gurnall could have had in his mind, but of course no one can say for sure whether he reasoned in this way. I can relate to this dilemma along with many others in the Church of England because by leaving we could abandon our flocks to false shepherds.

Ryle advances three other arguments in favour of Gurnall's action in agreeing to the Act of Uniformity. First, he says that Gurnall came into ministry during a period of English history when 'it was impossible to obtain Episcopal ordination and the use of the Prayer Book was almost forbidden'. He accepted things as they were, in difficult times. Second, there is no evidence that Gurnall had any problems with Episcopal ordination or the liturgy of the Church of England. When he agreed to the Act of Uniformity, he was (as far as we know), being consistent with what he had believed prior to this controversy. He had, as we would say, 'kept his head down in the parish' and had not got involved in the Westminster Assembly or public discussions as had Baxter and Owen. He had been, says Ryle, 'a quiet, retired preacher in a country parish, and there is really no proof whatever that his retention of his position at Lavenham was inconsistent with anything in his previous life'.

The final argument that Rye offers in defence of Gurnall's actions is that his diocesan bishop was Bishop Reynolds, 'himself a Puritan in doctrine and notoriously the most mild and lenient man on the Episcopal bench in dealing with scrupulous clergymen'. The character of his godly bishop may well have 'turned the scale' for Gurnall. Finally Ryle finishes his defence of Gurnall by suggesting that in movements like 1662 'the seceding party has not always a monopoly of grace and courage'. Ryle goes as far to say that in many cases like Gurnall's, 'I have no doubt, it showed more courage to submit to the Act of Conformity than to refuse submission, and in which it cost a man more to hold his living than throw it up'. I'm sure others would not be so positive as Ryle about Gurnall's actions and we may need reminding that much of Ryle's case is speculation and detective work, but I think his conclusions do throw a helpful light on both Gurnall's decision to remain in the Church of England and those of us who choose to do so today. Whether this is convincing will be for the reader to decide as Ryle says.

William Gurnall: A model for evangelicals today?

Paradoxically, William Gurnall may turn out to be just the example we need in the current situation of the Church in England. His story may be helpful to Anglican evangelicals who choose to remain and also for non-conformist evangelicals who wonder why godly evangelical men stay in the Church of England! I think Gurnall was someone willing to live with a messy situation yet willing to act bravely by staying in the Church of England for the very reasons J. I. Packer suggests in Chapter Nine, in order to preach the gospel and contend for the truth. Some will decide it is right for them to leave as Baxter did, whilst others will have no time for the Church of England at all, like Bunyan! I have good friends who take each of these positions. Whatever approach is taken by individuals one of the lessons of the Puritans is that we should try and show mutual support rather than express criticism and suspicion of each other. We need each other as evangelical folk. Let everyone be true to his own conscience but let there be generosity of spirit on all sides. Let's remember we will all be in heaven together!

A tendency to divide on secondary matters: an evangelical blindspot?

I raised Dallas Willard's devastating critique of the Western church in chapter five. I used the term 'Western church' because this is not just a feature of *the conservative side of the church today*. I have argued that a genuine faith will lead to holiness of life. It is essential for folk to experience regeneration as stressed by Boston and other Puritans which leads to union with Christ and this is our only basis of acceptance by God and leads to both new birth and a sanctified life. The Puritans rightly stressed holiness of life and Christlikeness as evidence for true conversion. All of this I think is plain both in the New Testament and in the faithful expression of it in the Puritans. However, as I have looked at the Puritans and at evangelicals today I have to conclude that we can easily mistake friends for enemies! Franklin D. Roosevelt, in a conversation with Winston Churchill in Yalta in 1945 is reputed to have said: 'One Pole is a charmer; two Poles—a brawl; three Poles—well, this is the Polish Question'.[138] I have Polish friends and I know how passionate they are! I have heard it said of evangelicals that there will be as many views on a particular subject as there are evangelicals in a room! Whilst it's right to be passionate about what we believe as evangelicals we do seem to have a blind spot about accepting each other on secondary matters! The Reformation slogan was 'In essentials, unity; in non-essentials, liberty; in all things, charity'. Romans 14 seems to be a good commentary on this although the heart of the problem is deciding what is essential!

We could take a lesson from Boston who admits he was 'much addicted to peace, and averse to controversy; though once engaged therein, I was set to go through with it'. We should take a lesson from the story of William Gurnall, who was a conforming Puritan and Richard Baxter who was a reluctant non-conformist who preached theological unity in a period of intense division. We should remember John Bunyan, who whilst being convinced of his Baptist views did not make them essential for church membership. Bishop J. C. Ryle wisely said in regard to secondary matters: 'Let us keep the hedges low between us so that we can easily lean over and shake hands'.

Its worth repeating Leith Anderson's helpful point made earlier: 'Those who strive to be New Testament churches must seek to live its principles and absolutes, not produce the details'. William Gurnall and others today who decide in good conscience to stay in the Church of England should work more closely together with those who share the core *principles and absolutes* of the New Testament and not fall out so often about its details. Those evangelicals outside the Church of England should seek to work with those inside it as conscience permits and show generosity of spirit as fellow workers in God's kingdom. Reminding ourselves of the perspective of heaven should have a sobering effect.

David Meager, writing in Crossway, a magazine produced by Church Society, has some interesting thoughts about Gurnall and those who remained in the Church of England in terms of a later revival and ministries blessed by God:

> As we reflect on 1662, we should give thanks to God that though weakened doctrinally and numerically at this time, 1662 was not the death of reformed doctrine in the established church as some might suggest. Through men like William Gurnall, the gospel was preserved for future generations. When revival arrived in the century following 1662 it was amongst the Anglican clergy where it took root first … and since then many have viewed the Anglican formularies as sufficiently reformed to exercise fruitful ministries within its structures. The ministries of

George Whitefield, Augustus Toplady, John Newton, Charles Simeon, Hugh Boyd McNeile, J. C. Ryle, Richard Hobson, Alan Stibbes, Dick Lucas and many others testify to this.[139]

William Gurnall's *The Christian in Complete Armour* is the record of this godly man's inner thoughts and his reflections on the spiritual battle. These thoughts must have been in his mind when he went through the fires of testing in 1662. He was no hypocrite! It is my contention backed up by Bishop Ryle and others that this man was no coward, but one moved by his vision of heaven. As he was struggling with his conscience submitted to the Scriptures he decided to go against the example of many of his friends and colleagues and remain in the Church of England. Subsequent history has proved that this was at least a valid option and perhaps a wise one. Let the reader decide.

Gurnall's vision of heaven in his eye caused him to make this difficult decision and face misunderstanding and even severe criticism from his fellow believers. I have been in such situations as I guess many fellow evangelicals have. As Gurnall went through this storm, his raft made up of the big picture of the Bible with its focus on the cross to save sinners and the promise of heaven to motivate saints sustained him during his trials. Many can testify to the same experience, that God takes his people though times of severe testing to make us better not bitter. Dallas Willard says that, 'A carefully cultivated heart will, assisted by the grace of God, foresee, forestall, or transform most of the painful situations before which others stand like helpless children saying "Why?"' In my experience the Puritans, including William Gurnall, can offer the means for transforming our souls to the glory of God and the blessing of others. They help us turn from the prevailing 'auxiliary' attitude of compromise to the more authentic 'legionnaire' thinking of serving manfully for the promise of heaven. This citizenship is for a far greater kingdom than Rome or any earthly blessing but membership of the Kingdom of God, which endures forever and transforms life on earth for the better. Simon Ponsonby speaks of the transforming effect of this citizenship of the kingdom of heaven.

> The 'Pax Romana' would be the Roman Empire's attempted social construct to unite the disparate nations that belonged to it, establishing unity under the emperor, but it is in fact only the kingdom of heaven through obedience to the shared gospel that can genuinely and freely unite Jew and Gentile under Christ.[140]

If this kingdom of heaven can unite Jew and Gentile under Christ, then surely it ought to unite gospel folk working for the same kingdom but finding themselves called to diverse situations: some in Anglican churches and some in non-conformist churches. I am convinced that Gurnall, Baxter and Boston would exhort us to unite as one band of brothers and sisters seeking first the kingdom of God and anticipating eternity, where together with all God's faithful people we will praise and worship the Lamb.

Section 3
The Need for a
Passionate Spirituality

13

Running to the tape:
The need for a passionate spirituality

Bunyan: *The Heavenly Footman* 1692

In these two remaining chapters I want to address the need for a passionate spirituality to enjoy a useful rather than a wasted life. We need to break away from the mediocrity we find all around us. The Puritans were unashamed enthusiasts who lived their lives to the full and had a cheerfulness that came from their doctrine of hope; they believed passionately that their lives had meaning and purpose since they were on a journey to heaven. Their focus on heaven helped release them from selfish concerns to seek holiness of life and service of others. We will see in these two chapters how that passion can be caught and then how it can be maintained and developed through life. I say 'caught' because these writers have acted as mentors to my soul and I have caught something of their spirit rather than just gained some useful knowledge. It's been like having my own personal trainer! We become like the people we admire. We will look at two things: a training regime requiring self-discipline that will help deliver this new quality of Christian experience and a mind-set that can overcome all obstacles including death, summed up by the phrase *dying to live.* It's my prayer that you will be blessed as much as I have been and that your Christian life will be lifted to a new level of experience. The Puritan mind is designed to develop a doctrine for living that enables believers to flourish in good times and bad. It produces a cultivated heart assisted by the transforming grace of God that gives us a passionate spirituality.

In chapter ten we considered Bunyan's masterpiece *Pilgrim's Progress,* through which he shot to fame and afterwards began a happy and established period of his life as a sought-after writer and pastor of a church in Bedford. We don't know when Bunyan wrote *The Heavenly Footman* but it was published in 1692, four years after his death and it is very likely it was written just after *Pilgrim's Progress* since it takes up the same themes of running as we saw in the first part of that book. A footman is not a foot soldier but someone who travels on foot. Christian says to Hopeful, 'Such footmen as thee and I are'. Whilst a footman is not a foot soldier we will continue our theme of Bunyan being a soldier-pilgrim. Running is something soldiers regularly do in training and it is something soldiers need to be able to do on the battlefield itself. Running is also something done by athletes. Bunyan takes up his text of 1 Corinthians 9:24 'So run that you may obtain,' with the same passion that we see in *Pilgrim's Progress*: exhorting believers to run to the tape, the finish line of heaven with a passion, avoiding all distractions and keeping heaven in their eye and earth on their heart. I was a PE teacher and I know about training for sporting success.

Let Bunyan be your personal trainer providing you with the training regime you need to get going and keep going. We all need a passionate spirituality.

If sport leaves you cold then remember what Paul says in 1 Timothy 4:8,

> for while bodily training is of some value, godliness is of value in every way, as it holds promise for the present life and also for the life to come.

It's spiritual training for the present and the future that Bunyan is concerned about in *The Heavenly Footman*, not sport for its own sake. The two paintings of Bunyan in later life show him as quite rotund, which is quite reassuring for me considering my present physical shape!

The Heavenly Footman is an extended sermon on 1 Corinthians 9:24–26.

> Do you not know that in a race all the runners run, but only one receives the prize? So run that you may obtain it. Every athlete exercises self-control in all things. They do it to receive a perishable wreath, but we an imperishable. So I do not run aimlessly; I do not box as one beating the air.

A spiritual check-up

When I went along to my local gym some years ago (and I urgently need to go back!) they began by giving me a physical check-up: recording my weight and height, blood pressure etc. Then the coach explained what the function of each piece of apparatus was and how it could be used to develop specific things like strength, endurance and so on. We need a regular spiritual check-up to keep us running to the tape with a passionate spirituality.

W. E. Sangster, in the daily readings book I was given as a young Christian has a list of diagnostic questions under the title *The Passing Years* ...

How long is it since I became a Christian?

Have I grown steadily with the years?

Was I ever further forward than I am now?

Can I measure my progress in the last ten years? Five years? Twelve months?

I wonder how much of life remains?

What can I do now that I could not do five years ago?

Lead another person to Christ?

Distinguish guidance from my own desires?

Forgive those who have wronged me?

Look death in the face?

This check-up is very challenging but very helpful and is best done on a yearly basis. Sangster mentions the maturity to

Look death in the face and we will look at the issue of death in the final chapter of the book. Here we will focus on Bunyan's fitness regime in *The Heavenly Footman*, which pictures the Christian life like a foot race where we need to keep our eyes on the finishing line of heaven and run with passion.

> Beg of God that he will do two things for thee: First, enlighten thine understanding. And, second, inflame thy will. If these two be but effectually done, there is no fear but thou will go to heaven. Enlighten thine understanding. One of the great reasons why men and women do so little regard the other world, it is because they see so little of it.

Bunyan says the people of the world have their understanding darkened. (Ephesians 4:17–18)

> Walk not as those, run not with them. Cry to the Lord for enlightening grace and say, Lord, open my blind eyes, Lord take the veil off my dark heart, show me the things of the other world, and let me see the sweetness, glory and excellency of them for Christ's sake.[141]

As we saw earlier in Boston and Baxter, Bunyan points to the necessity of the new birth that leads to the normal Christian life: a passionate spirituality. He warns of the danger of hardening hearts to the grace of God instead of seeking it continually. As the sinner cries to God for enlightening grace, their eyes are opened and they see the reality of the *other world*. This new vision of heaven transforms their life on earth. Their minds are enlightened so that they can say with Paul, 'our citizenship is in heaven, and from it we await a Saviour, the Lord Jesus Christ' (Philippians 3:20).

Critical to healthy growth as a Christian is to move from head-knowledge to heart-knowledge and the engagement of the will. Bunyan's second instruction as our spiritual coach is,

> Inflame thy will. Cry to God that he would inflame thy will also with the things of the other world ... Indeed to have such a will for heaven, is an admirable advantage to a man that undertakes the race thither ...

Bunyan says Jacob and Job both testify to the benefit of this: 'I will not let you go except thou bless me' (Genesis 32:26); 'though he slay me, yet will I trust in him' (Job 13:15). Bunyan comments: 'Oh this blessed inflamed will for heaven!'[142]

We need inflamed wills to give us a passionate spirituality. David Brainerd who went as a missionary to the Native Americans wrote in his journal: 'If I cannot serve God one way I will serve him another—I will never leave off this blessed service'. Christ had captured his heart: has he captured yours and mine? Otherwise our service is just drudge and duty like the elder son in the parable Jesus told in Luke 15. 'With a captivated heart our service will be duty and delight'.[143]

This delight—or what I am calling a passionate spirituality—will sustain us in time of extreme pressure to follow our conscience and do our duty. Bunyan brings as witnesses [the] saints of old, they being willing, and resolved for heaven, what could stop them? Could fire or faggot, sword or halter, stinking dungeons, whips, bears, bulls, lions, cruel rackings, stoning, starving, nakedness (Hebrews 11 and Romans 8:27) … Oh therefore cry hard to God to inflame thy will for heaven and for Christ … Get thy will tipt with heavenly grace, and resolution against discouragements, and then thou goest full speed for heaven.[144]

'Lord, give your church today such a passion for heaven!'

Strip, ready for a spiritual workout

Here we have strong echoes of *Pilgrims Progress* and my experience of the gym!

'Take all in short in this little piece of paper'. (My coach gave me a weekly list of specific exercises including how many and for how long and made sure I was doing them properly!)

Get into the way. Then study on it. Then strip, and lay aside everything that would hinder. Beware of by-paths. Do not gaze or stare too much about thee, and be sure to ponder the path of thy feet. Do not stop for any that call after thee, whether it be the world, the flesh or the devil; for all these will hinder your journey, if possible. Be not daunted with any discouragements, thou meetest with as thou goest. Take heed of stumbling at the cross. Cry hard to God for an enlightened heart, and a willing mind, and God give thee a prosperous journey.[145]

If you look at most 100-metre runners from the play-back from behind the finish tape they never look from side to side but they concentrate on the finishing line. I say 'most' because having watched the 'lightning bolt' on a recorded 100-metre

race of the 2012 Olympic final, when he set a new Olympic
record, Bolt is looking at the clock to see his time! But I am sure
you get the point Bunyan is making: we are to be single-minded
about keeping our gaze on heaven's gate. We are to strip and
lay aside everything that hinders (Hebrews 12:1). We are not
to look away and we are not to stop for anyone! This applies
to the training that goes into preparation for athletic races
and for the races themselves. Such athletes put everything into
achieving success. As a sports teacher I was trained to encourage
all children to do their best and that 'taking part is what's most
important'. That may be correct at school level, but these top
athletes like Bolt take part to win—and so should we!

When I was a young minister, an older vicar gave me
some valuable advice when he said, 'Don't be discouraged
by discouragement'. Another church leader said, 'Roll with
the punches!' I wondered what they meant at the time, but I
know now! Bunyan expresses the same advice by saying, 'Be
not daunted with any discouragements'. At theological college
no one taught a class on what some psychologists are calling
today *emotional intelligence*: perhaps they do today. It is vital
in Christian ministry to be emotionally resilient in order to
cope with the almost relentless negativity you can experience
in Christian work. A recognition that such discouragement
is a reality, and that a single-minded gaze at heaven's gate is a
great antidote to restore emotional and spiritual balance and
perspective, should be mandatory teaching at all institutions
training folk for the pastoral ministry. Perhaps if there was a focus
on building emotional intelligence (E.I.) during such training
there might be a lower drop-out rate amongst clergy and fewer
cases of burnout or moral failure. Whilst you need to avoid the

psycho-babble and new age philosophy of so called 'holistic training' involving complementary therapies, self-help, coaching, management, New Age and spiritual fields, I believe all truth is God's truth and modern psychology may provide help in self-understanding and awareness as well as understanding others in terms of their emotional life. This help could be invaluable for pastors and others working in churches.

Edinburgh University offers an undergraduate course which promises:

> This course will review the main topics in research on human emotions and some recent findings on individual differences in emotional dispositions and capabilities. The review of emotions research will include: definition and function of emotions, basic and complex emotions, dimensional and categorical models of emotion, emotion perception, models of emotion-processing, social aspects of emotions. The individual differences topics will centre on the relatively new construct of emotional intelligence (EI), but will also include other individual difference approaches, for example personality/affect relationships, emotion regulation, and coping. The coverage of EI will include controversies relating to its existence and measurement, for example whether it is more appropriate to view EI as part of the intelligence or the personality domain.

Motivation is all

Emotion also plays a large part in what motivates us towards transformational change.

It's one thing to get to the gym, it's another to keep going when it hurts or is inconvenient. There are almost 4.5 million adults in the UK who have a gym membership, an increase of almost a million since 2000 but only 27% go regularly to the gym. This is good news for the owners of gyms but not for those paying membership fees! To get fit physically and remain in good shape requires motivation—not just signing up and spending money. I am thinking about joining *Slimming World* to lose a lot of excess weight. I say *thinking* because so far I haven't summoned up the courage to go along to the local centre. I think the motivational techniques of such approaches are both positive and negative. The positive is to offer delicious food that leaves you feeling full rather than empty. The negative element is to motivate you to keep to the diet and exercise to avoid a weekly public humiliation! Bunyan points to both positive and negative motives to keep heaven in our eye.

Motives to make us passionate about our faith

He lists nine: I will mention four:

The First Motive
Consider there is no way but this, thou must either win or lose (heaven)

There cannot be anything more important than to get to heaven by winning the prize. Bunyan is basing his extended sermon in *The Heavenly Footman* on 1 Corinthians 9:24–26. Paul contrasts in verse 25 the athlete's giving their all to win a fading earthly reward compared to the Christian giving their all for the reward that is eternal: *They do it to receive a perishable wreath, but we an imperishable.*

The Second Motive

Consider that this devil, this hell, death and damnation, followeth after thee as hard as they can drive, and have their commission so to do by the law, against which thou hast sinned; and therefore for the Lord's sake make haste.

If the devil and his minions are passionate about what they do, how much more should be the children of the light!

The Fourth Motive

Know also, that now heaven's gates, the heart of Christ, with his arms, are wide open to receive thee.

Just as the trainer waits by the finish line to congratulate the runner, so Christ waits in heaven to welcome the Christian.

The Fifth Motive

Keep thine eye upon the prize; be sure that thy eyes be continually upon the profit thou art like to get. Most lose heaven for want of considering the price and the worth of it … [Therefore], *keep thine eye much upon the excellency, the sweetness, the beauty, the comfort, the peace, that is to be had there by those that win the prize.* It was this prize, Bunyan says, that made the Apostle run through all the sufferings he endured, and the saints since. Don't be put off by the idea that heaven is too good for you. *Heaven is prepared for whosoever will accept it, and they shall be entertained with hearty good welcome … Therefore take heart And run, man.*[146]

All these motives taken together make a compelling case for seeking heaven, above all things with a passion! Like the long-distance runner we are to keep our eyes on the prize: Bunyan refs to the cost that is well worth the price because of 'the beauty, the comfort, the peace'. Most attractive of all is the picture he paints of Christ with arms 'wide open to receive thee'. Heaven's doors stand open to receive all who will win the race.

Uses (Application)

Puritan preaching was not only good at exposition but it also showed people how to live according to the truth that was being taught: a doctrine for life. Most evangelical preaching is weak on application. When you experience Puritan application, what they called 'Uses', you will see the need to carefully apply the word to the various categories of listeners. There is often a wide range of spiritual states gathered in our church meetings: the unconverted needing to be born anew, new Christians who need the milk of the word, older saints needing meat, as well as folk experiencing a wide range of circumstances from happiness to extreme suffering. The Puritans took the trouble to address a wide range of spiritual states, but then their sermons were much longer than evangelical sermons today. Matthew Henry, an exceptional preacher spent an hour on exposition and an hour on 'uses'. His commentary on the whole Bible remains very helpful and accessible today both for understanding a passage and applying it to daily life. Bunyan in *The Heavenly Footman* applies his teaching on running to heaven in nine points of application. These we can sum up as self-examination and struggle.

(1) Examine yourself honestly

Art thou got into the right way? Art thou in Christ's righteousness? Do not say yes in thy hart, when in truth there is no such matter. It is a dangerous thing, you know, for a man to think he is in the right way, when he is wrong ... Oh this is the misery of most men, to persuade themselves that they run right, when they never had one foot in the way! The Lord give thee understanding here, or else thou art undone for ever.[147]

Make sure, warns Bunyan, that you are running on the right path because the heart is deceitful. Bunyan asks searching questions to probe our relationship to Christ:

> Do you see yourself in him? Is he the more precious to you than the whole world? Is your mind always thinking about him? Do you love talking about him and also walking with him? Does his company sweeten all things—and his absence embitter all things?

I said in chapter four, about the Bible and heaven, that the thing that will make heaven, heaven, will be the presence of Jesus. Dallas Willard helpfully stresses that we need heaven in believers and not just believers in heaven. If we love Jesus then this will help bring part of heaven to earth. Such an intimate fellowship with Christ will give us a passionate spirituality that not only looks forward to being forever with the Lord but extending his kingdom here on earth.

(2) Be prepared for struggle

In chapter one I said that many people have swallowed the false notion that becoming a Christian is meant to make your life easier. Perhaps it's the fault of some evangelists in not stressing the cost of taking up the cross and following Jesus. Bunyan and the Puritans are biblical realists who teach us by word and personal example that the Christian life is meant to be tough. It will mean a fight and a struggle.

> To run through all that opposition, all these jostles, all these rubs, over all these stumbling blocks, over all these snares from all these entanglements, that the devil, sin, the world, and thine own heart, lay before the; I tell thee, if thou art agoing heavenward, thou wilt find it no small or easy matter …

Do not be among the many that, 'will seek to enter and will not be able' (Luke 13:24).

Take warning from those who

> seemed to outstrip many, but now are running as fast back again … Oh sad! What doom they will have, who were almost at heaven's gates, and then run back again … And if not fit for the kingdom of heaven then for certain he must needs be fit for the fire of hell (Hebrews 10:38).[148]

To those who have been Christians a long time, he warns lest the

> young striplings of Jesus, that began to strip but the other day, do not outrun you, so that as to have that scripture fulfilled in you, 'The first shall be last, and the last first' … I say, strive to outrun them.[149]

Hurrah, there is such a thing as godly competition! There speaks a former PE teacher!

Beware of lazy professors:

> Some men profess themselves such as run for heaven as well
> as any; yet [they are], lazy, slothful, cold, half-hearted … It cost
> the foolish virgins dear for coming too late (Matthew 25:10–12)
> … [And], How was Lot's wife served for running lazily, and
> for giving but one look behind her, after the things she left in
> Sodom? How as Esau served for staying too long before he came
> for the blessing?[150]

These things are written for our learning:

> For whatever was written in former days was written for
> our instruction, that through endurance and through the
> encouragement of the Scriptures we might have hope (Romans
> 15:4).

Bunyan's application is summed up by him in one sentence:
'Run consistently to make best use of the time you have, "and
so run that thou mayest obtain"'. We in the church today
would do well to listen and apply these 'uses'. Dallas Willard
is right when he says our main problem in terms of healthy
discipleship is *simple distraction*. The Puritans can act as our
personal trainers to keep us running to the tape by staying
focused on what's important.

As well as the general danger of simple distraction there are
specific periods of life that will offer more danger of coasting
or even giving up the race, even if we are still attending church!
In the Western world there is a period called 'midlife crisis',
which seems to particularly afflict men but can also affect some

women. This can happen when a certain level has been reached in a career and no further promotion seems possible. It can happen when youthful energies begin to slacken and a general weariness can set in. It can of course be due to loss of job or breakdown in marriage in mid-life which can affect both sexes. The feeling that certain goals have not been achieved or rewards experienced, can also lead to a deep sense of disillusionment. It can happen when children leave the home, the so called 'empty nest syndrome'.

Bunyan and the Puritans would say in response to these distractions and complex challenges that as Christians we must keep heaven in our eye and earth on our heart. If we aim at heaven we will get earth thrown in; if we aim at earth, where many of the above issues are focused, we will get neither!

A danger period for Christian young people is the transition from school to the freedom of university. Since I was converted during my teacher-training that did not apply to me but I have known several Christian students who had great struggles. Another important point is when folk leave university and set up in a career, perhaps a long way from their Christian parents and supportive churches. Later on a specific danger can come at the point of retirement from paid employment. The temptation for the Christian who is focused on this world is to see their remaining thirty plus years as time to just enjoy themselves rather than continuing to serve God and others. Of course not everyone is able to retire, especially as we are living longer in the West and more people need to work to an older age. There are others, particularly in the professions who become financially comfortable and are tempted to see the rest of their lives as one long self-indulgent holiday! Bunyan and the Puritans would say this is to waste our lives and forget we should be on the road to heaven. He ends his book with a strong exhortation to run to heaven with every fibre of our being.

A final word of challenge to run

Well, then, sinner, what sayest thou? Where is thy heart? Wilt thou run? Art thou resolved to strip? ... Think quickly, man, it is no dallying in this matter. Confer not with flesh and blood; look up to heaven, and see how thou likest it; also to hell ... If thou dost not know the way, inquire of the Word of God. If thou wantest company, cry for God's Spirit. If thou wantest encouragement, entertain the promises. But be sure thou begin by times; get into the way; run apace and hold out to the end: and the Lord give thee a prosperous journey. Farewell.[151]

Every year Carlisle hosts the Great North Run, and the runners go right past our church just before our morning service starts. I always watch for a few minutes. At the front of the race there are the keen ones with resolve to win written on their faces! Then there are the 'jokers' dressed up in wonderfully bright costumes who are doing it for fun. They are not trying to win the race; they are just taking part to enjoy themselves! Some folk who come to church are like that today. They just come to enjoy themselves and meet their own needs rather than to be passionate disciples. Bunyan would say to such folk, 'Get in the race, and race to win the prize of eternal life'. In the Christian race there can be more than one winner—in fact we can all win—but it's also possible to fail to finish. We need to run well, right to the tape, with a passionate spirituality. That's my ambition and I hope you share it.

14

Dying to live: Recovering Radical Discipleship

Baxter: *The Saints' Everlasting Rest* 1650

Dietrich Bonhoeffer wrote in *The Cost of Discipleship*, 'When Christ calls a man, he bids him come and die'. Bonhoeffer lived in a period of German history when it was very costly to be an authentic Christian. There were many in the German church who compromised their faith in favour of security and materialism and supported Hitler. Nazism was a pseudo-religion where the Führer was worshipped as a god. Bonhoeffer and the Confessing Church were prepared to risk persecution and death because of their opposition to this wicked ideology that was deeply opposed to authentic Christianity. Marxism is equally opposed to the gospel and hates Christ. In the Twentieth century more Christians were killed for their faith than in all the previous centuries put together. From what we have seen so far in this century this trend is continuing, especially in parts of the Middle-East and Africa. In the West we are confronted by a militant atheism that often expresses itself in a soft-Marxism. Where this will lead it is hard to predict but already a succession of street preachers have been arrested in the UK but not charged. These pernicious forces within our society, whilst clearly not on the same trajectory as Hitler's Nazism or Stalin's Marxism, are determined to remove Christianity from our public square and national life. As in Hitler's Germany and Stalin's Russia, Christians in the West are under mounting pressure to compromise their faith in favour of the prevailing culture. We have reached a critical turning point.

It has been the thesis of this book that the Puritans can give evangelicals resources to thrive spiritually in these difficult times by keeping heaven in our eye and earth on our heart. In chapter thirteen we saw how the Puritans can ignite a passionate spirituality that can combat nominalism, helping us run the Christian race faithfully to the end of our lives. In this final chapter we will see how the Puritans can release us from the fear of death and enable us to look forward to death as the entrance into our promised rest. We will find these resources by looking at Richard Baxter's *The Saints' Everlasting Rest.* Since Puritans like Baxter were Calvinists we will examine Calvin's view of meditating on the future life. Two opposite extremes are to be avoided: those who refuse to see the good purposes of God in the troubles of this life and simply want to die early; and those timid and faithless Christians who fear and tremble at the prospect of death. We will consider those who have problems with life and those who have problems with death and ask whether Baxter and Calvin are united in their approach.

1. Problems with life: exile and prison

Baxter sees heaven as *our country*, when he prays at the beginning of his book: 'It must be the business of our lives, to have heaven continually in our eye'.[152]

He argues forcibly that we must ask our consciences whether we have set eternal rest before the eyes of our friends and relations or not? Have 'we watched and laboured with all our might that no man take our crown?' For Baxter, as for all the Puritans, heaven is the destination that must shape the journey. But did Baxter in seeing heaven as the business of our lives, see the earth simply as a place of exile? He asks: 'Does it become the Christian to expect so much here? Our rest is in heaven'.

Interestingly, Baxter refers to the three Puritan motifs we have used in this book of shepherd-captain, soldier and pilgrim. He uses each to illustrate that the journey is not the saints' rest: the mariner does not choose to remain on the sea, the soldier does not rest in the midst of his enemies and the pilgrim wants to complete his journey, and 'are not Christians such travellers, such mariners, such soldiers?'[153]

We saw in chapter two how Calvin seems to be world-rejecting in his famous quote: 'If heaven is our country, what can the earth be but a place of exile?'[154]

Baxter continually refers to the wilderness of this world, a term for a place of exile and wandering. He pictures himself on a mountain where he is able to see both earth and heaven:

To stand on that mount, whence we can see the wilderness

and Canaan both at once—to stand in heaven and look back on earth, and weigh them together in the balance of a comparing sense and judgment.[155]

In a chapter entitled *It is not on earth, (that is not our ultimate rest)* he warns the soul that would rather stay in exile:

> O unworthy soul, who hadst rather dwell in this land of darkness, and wander in this barren wilderness, than be at rest with Jesus Christ; who hadst rather stay among the wolves, and daily suffer the scorpion's stings, than praise the Lord with the host of heaven.[156]

The pilgrim, like the Israelites in the Wilderness is to 'be much in feeding on the hidden manna and frequently tasting the delights of heaven'.[157]

In a chapter on the subject of a heavenly life on earth lived as an exile he writes,

> If you were banished into a strange land, how frequently would your thoughts be at home. And why is it not thus with regard to heaven? Is not that more properly our home, where we must take up our heavenly abode, than this, which we are every hour expecting to be separated from, and to see no more? We are strangers, and that is our country. We are heirs, and that is our inheritance.[158]

Baxter and Calvin have the same view of life as an exile from heaven. However when we see Calvin's statement quoted above about the earth being 'but a place of exile' in its context, a different perspective emerges:

> If heaven is our country, what can the earth be but a place of exile? If departure from the world is entrance into life, what is the world but a sepulchre, and what is residence in it but immersion in death? If to be freed from the body is to gain full possession of freedom, what is the body but a prison? If it is the very summit of happiness to enjoy the presence of God, is it not miserable to want it? But 'whilst we are at home in the body, we are absent from the Lord,' (2 Corinthians 5:6). Thus when the earthly is compared with the heavenly life, it may undoubtedly be despised and trampled under foot. We ought never, indeed, to regard it with hatred, except in so far as it keeps us subject to sin; and even this hatred ought not to be directed against life itself.[159]

The context of the chapter is that Calvin is dealing with those facing the sufferings of life who simply want to die early! A few sentences earlier he writes of those 'who thought, that the best thing was not to be born, the next best to die early. For, being destitute of the light of God and of true religion, what could they see in it that was not of dire and evil omen?' He is saying don't regard life with hatred even if it feels like a continuous exile or like being in prison compared to the blessing of heaven. We are to see the good purposes of God in the sufferings of life and hate neither life, nor God! As we have seen throughout the book, God allows us to experience the troubles and vanities of life to help us reject the world and seek Christ and heaven as our only hope. Calvin strikes a balance between the Christian's total contempt for the world compared to heaven, and thankfulness for earth's blessings. These blessings are to lead us to God and give us an appetite for heaven.

Are Calvin and Baxter ascetics?

The Dictionary.com defines an ascetic as 'a person who practises great self-denial and austerities and abstains from worldly comforts and pleasures, especially for religious reasons'. Calvin and the Puritans did not reject the good things of God's creation but saw heaven as their home. For them the creation is to be enjoyed, but not to the detriment of the soul. The physical creation, according to Calvin, reflects the greatness and goodness of God, for the creation itself is good. 'Meanwhile, being placed in this most beautiful theatre, let us not decline to take a pious delight in the clear and manifest works of God'.[160]

Calvin is no ascetic. His encouragement is to enjoy the world as God's good gift but not lose our souls to it.

Baxter, like Calvin, dismisses temporal blessings as unimportant only in the light of the superior blessings of heaven: Calvin talks about temporal blessings 'in comparison with future immortality, let us despise life'. Baxter's concern, like Calvin's, is that good things can prevent us seeking the best: 'When we enjoy convenient houses, goods, lands, and revenues, or the necessary means God hath appointed for our spiritual good, we seek rest in these enjoyments'. So there are legitimate earthly pleasures and joys but the potential snare is to 'mistake them for our rest ... The most dangerous mistake of our souls is, to take the creature for God, and earth for heaven'.[161]

Having earth on his heart as well as heaven in his eye, Calvin was also interested in transforming the world by the grace of God.

Rather than withdrawal from the world, Calvin called for involvement. 'To Calvin the redeeming work of Christ was meant to transform the world and therefore spirituality was meant to serve Christ in the world'.[162] We have seen in this book how the Puritans following Calvin had a comprehensive view of life that sought to bring holiness to every aspect of life on earth, fulfilling Dallas Willard's concern that we should not simply seek to get people into heaven but heaven into people. We've also seen a continuity of theology throughout the book with a concern about regeneration leading to union with Christ that leads to this transformation. We have noticed this in the theology of Boston, Baxter and Bunyan. Its roots were in Calvin, who wrote:

> The ultimate goal is a perfect union with God. In union with Christ we become one with him. 'Therefore, to that union of the head and members, the residence of Christ in our hearts, in fine a mystical union we assign the highest rank.'[163]

2. Problems with death: denying or defying death?

In our culture we are in denial about our mortality, and much of the church is no different from the world. Many believers are professing faith in Christ but living almost like Marxists! This is reflected in our compromise to the prevailing culture and by our refusal to face up to the fact of death. Fear of death is not a new problem: the Renaissance philosopher, François de La Rochefoucauld, spoke for many people when he wrote, 'Neither the sun nor death can be looked at steadily'. Baxter did look at death steadily because he had a Puritan mind with heaven in his eye and earth on his heart. It gave him spiritual resources, 'a cultivated heart', to thrive in the most adverse of circumstances, as we saw in chapters nine and eleven. Bonhoeffer had discovered the secret of radical discipleship, 'dying to live', and so had Baxter. Richard Baxter did not have a strong constitution. Having to sleep rough out in the fields with the Commonwealth Army during the civil war took a terrible toll on his health. He was taken in by kind friends, Sir Thomas and Lady Rous, who nursed him back to health. Believing that he was dying, he wrote *The Saints' Everlasting Rest* for his own soul, about the importance of heaven and how to get there. He had no other book but an open Bible but he was strongly influenced by John Calvin, as were all the Puritans. Calvin helped them to defy death rather than deny its existence.

Baxter shows that he has no longing for death, in and for itself, but is someone who longs to have a closer relationship with his God. Death is a means to that end of having perfect union with Christ in heaven.

'I confess that death, of itself, is not desirable; but the soul's rest with God is, to which death is the common passage'.[164]

Death is the means to eternal life and so as Paul says, 'while we are at home in the body we are away from the Lord'. To be with the Lord is far better, yet our human nature makes us want to linger like Lot in Sodom, expressing what Baxter calls 'our unreasonable unwillingness to die, that we may possess the Saint's rest'. This Baxter calls a sin, which we are 'apt to make light of ... Though there is much faith and Christianity in our mouths, yet there is much infidelity and paganism in our hearts, which is the chief cause that we are so loath to die'.

We are reluctant to embrace death because our love for Christ is cold, comments Baxter. We show no passion to be with him but content ourselves with earth's pleasures and loves. By 'our unwillingness to die, it appears we are little weary with sin ... and insensible to the vanity of earth, when we are so loath to hear or think of a removal'.[165] He returns to the analogy used earlier of the mariner, soldier and pilgrim but adds others: 'Does not the husbandman desire the harvest, and the labourer receive his pay? Doth the traveller long to be at home, and the racer to win the prize?' His conclusion is that 'we may reconcile ourselves to the world, but it will never reconcile itself to us'.

Then he makes a shocking statement:

> This unwillingness to die doth actually impeach us of high treason against the Lord. Is it not choosing earth before him, and taking present things for our happiness, and consequently making them our very god? ... Would you have any believe you when you call the Lord your only hope, and speak of Christ as all in all, and of the joy that is in his presence, and yet would endure the hardest life, rather than die and enter into his presence?

Is our reluctance to embrace death high treason? Baxter states the matter plainly once again: 'For a member of Christ and an heir of heaven to be afraid of entering his own inheritance, is a sinful, useless fear'. This is strong meat, perhaps as challenging as when Jesus says in John 6:53–54 'Truly, truly, I say to you, unless you eat the flesh of the Son of Man and drink his blood, you have no life in you. Whoever feeds on my flesh and drinks my blood has eternal life, and I will raise him up on the last day'. John records the negative reaction to these words of Jesus, 'many of his disciples turned back and no longer walked with him' (v66).

What does Calvin teach about death?

Wherefore, if it becomes us to live and die to the Lord, let us leave the period of our life and death at his disposal. Still let us ardently long for death, and constantly meditate upon it, and in comparison with future immortality, let us despise life, and, on account of the bondage of sin, long to renounce it whenever it shall so please the Lord. But, most strange to say, many who boast of being Christians, instead of thus longing for death, are so afraid of it that they tremble at the very mention of it as a thing ominous and dreadful.[166]

Both Baxter and Calvin have uncompromising views of how to handle death. Perhaps they both reflect a secure upbringing that enabled them to be so emphatic?

Baxter wrote about death when he thought himself dying and perhaps this made his book more uncompromising than it would have been if he had wrote it in good health.

John Bunyan, who had an unhappy childhood and struggled with depression, shows us a more pastoral approach in *Pilgrim's Progress*, when he pictures Christian and Hopeful crossing the river of death to the celestial city. Nearing their longed-for destination Christian and Hopeful find themselves by the Dark River, a wide and fast flowing stream. They look around for a bridge or boat to help them cross safely but some Shining Ones appear who tell them that they must cross the river themselves and that it is a test of faith, since those with faith have nothing to fear. Hopeful enters and finds a firm place to cross but Christian soon flounders in deep water which goes over his head making him think he will drown and never see the celestial city. Bunyan writes that, 'great darkness and horror fell on Christian, so that he could not see before him'. Hopeful goes to Christian's rescue, just as John Newton did for William Cowper, pulling Cowper back several times from attempts to take his own life (as mentioned earlier). When he eventually died peacefully, it was Cowper's young cousin who acted like Hopeful did for Christian in the Dark River. Dr Gaius Davies describes the death-bed scene thus: 'Johnny had not realized that his beloved Cowper had died until he noticed his expression had settled into one "of calmness and composure, mingled, as it were, with a holy surprise"'.[167]

Those who benefit from a relatively secure and loving upbringing can be ignorant of the fact that many people are broken inside like Cowper. It took me many years to realize this. Perhaps, I would prefer a Boston or a Bunyan at my bedside in my hour of death, rather than a Calvin or a Baxter, although all four men had the same view of heaven in your eye, and earth on your heart. They all believed that we should not fear death but embrace it when it is God's call to our heavenly home.

The circumstances of our death may affect the way we deal with it.

Some exceptional men, like Hopeful in *Pilgrim's Progress* and
Dietrich Bonhoeffer, may stride confidently across the Dark
River and by their example support many others who perhaps
feel more fearful, like Christian finding their feet slipping and
experiencing great darkness when the time comes to cross.
Bonhoeffer had no Hopeful or Johnny to help him over the
Dark River, but he was able to approach his unjust and cruel
death with calmness and dignity. In a *Memoir* by Gerhard
Leibholz, Bonhoeffer's Christian brother-in-law (married to his
twin sister), he describes Bonhoeffer's arrest, interrogation and
execution by the Gestapo:

> Bonhoeffer (together with his sister Christel and her husband,
> Hans von Dohnanyi) was arrested by the Gestapo in the house
> of his parents on April 5th, 1943. In prison and concentration
> camps, Bonhoeffer greatly inspired by his indomitable courage,
> his unselfishness and his goodness, all those who came in contact
> with him ... In his hearing before the Gestapo during his
> imprisonment, defenseless and powerless ... only fortified by
> the word of God in his heart, he stood erect and unbroken
> before his tormentors. He refused to recant, and defied the
> Gestapo machine by openly admitting that, as a Christian, he
> was an implacable enemy of [Hitler's] National Socialism and
> its totalitarian demands toward the citizen—defied it, although
> he was continually threatened with torture and with the arrest
> of his parents, his sisters and his fiancée ... Bonhoeffer, who was
> never tried, went steadfastly on his last way to be hanged, and
> died with admirable calmness and dignity.[168]

I don't know how I will react, as Hopeful or as Christian, when the time comes for my death. All I know is that God will be there to sustain me through this final test before entering the Celestial City. For most of us in the West it will be a death in hospital. Recently, I had an operation to sort out a slipped disc. The surgeon met with me beforehand and told me the usual news that I could die during the operation or be paralysed from the neck down! Waiting in the prep room immediately before the operation I felt a wonderful sense of God's presence. The theatre sister said as she wheeled me in, 'You are the most relaxed person I've ever had in surgery!' I replied that I was very much at peace because 'If anything did go wrong I know where I am going'. Of course, this is nothing like Bonhoeffer or Faithful in *Pilgrims Progress*. When I awoke from the anaesthetic apparently I pointed to my wife and said, 'She's the one I want!' but I don't really remember. Whilst I love my wife very much, better if my first words out of the anaesthetic were: 'Jesus Christ is the one I want!' Baxter cites a pious old minister quoting Socrates who

> rejoiced that he should die, because he believed he should see Homer, Hesiod, and other eminent persons. 'How much more do I rejoice', said the old man, 'who am to see Christ my Saviour, the eternal Son of God, in his assumed flesh; besides so many renowned patriarchs, prophets and apostles'.[169]

Baxter and Calvin have the same view of death as the entrance to eternal rest. It is not something to be denied but embraced, since it will lead us to heaven. Not only that, but it will empower us on earth. Baxter proved this: his daily practice of meditating on heaven for half an hour before bed sustained him through chronic ill health and a very busy and effective ministry.

What does the Bible and Church history say about our earthly pilgrimage?

It is fair to say that down through the history of the world the pilgrims have marched. Abraham, the first of the great pilgrims, the David's, the Jeremiahs, the Peters, the Johns, the Polycarps, the Augustines, the Tyndales, the Husses, the Luthers, the Calvins, the Whitefields, the Martins, the Livingstons, the Hudson Taylors, and so on down through the years. 'In sacred and unbroken succession,' to use the phrase that F. B. Meyer has used, 'They made the great confession that they were strangers and pilgrims on the earth.'

Not only is the church depicted as *strangers and pilgrims on earth,* the Lord Jesus was also an exile:

> Jesus is the Heavenly Sojourner, travelling through the foreign land of this fallen world to the eternal inheritance he came to possess by way of the cross. He came to inherit the world, by passing through the world and finishing the work of redemption.[170]

A letter to Diognetus written at the end of the fourth century says:

> Christians are indistinguishable from other men either by nationality, language or customs. They do not inhabit separate cities of their own, or speak a strange dialect, or follow some outlandish way of life ... With regard to dress, food and manner

of life in general, they follow the customs of whatever city they happen to be living in, whether it is Greek or foreign ... And yet there is something extraordinary about their lives. They live in their own countries as though they were only passing through. They play their full role as citizens, but labour under all the disabilities of aliens. Any country can be their homeland, but for them their homeland, wherever it may be, is a foreign country ... They pass their days upon earth, but they are citizens of heaven.[171]

These words could have been written about the Puritans, in terms of them being exiles on earth yet playing a full part in society, apart from their tendency to wear distinctive plain dress and their willingness to stand up for biblical teaching! The most important shared characteristic with their fellow Christians in the fourth century was that there was *something extraordinary about their lives.* They had a passionate spirituality that enabled them to flourish in good and bad circumstances with a Christ-like cheerfulness, even when facing death. We need their example and encouragement today to break out of our mediocrity and angst to find resources to flourish spiritually based on heaven in our eye and earth on our heart.

Endnotes

Chapter 1

1. Lemony Snicket, *The Wide Window* (London: Egmont Books, 2000) page 214.

2. Dallas Willard, *Renovation of the Heart* (Leicester: IVP, 2002) page 2.

3. C.S. Lewis, *Mere Christianity* (London: Harper Collins, 1952) page 134.

4. Thomas Boston, *The Crook in the Lot* (Edinburgh: Banner of Truth) page 8.

5. Ibid. page 12.

6. Obadiah Sedgwick, *Providence Handled Practically* (Grand Rapids: Reformation Heritage, 2007), page 7.

7. Richard Sibbes, *Bruised Reed, Works*, Volume 1 (Edinburgh: Banner of Truth, 1973) page 40.

8. Philip Graham Ryken, *Thomas Boston as Preacher of the Fourfold State* (Edinburgh: Paternoster, 1999) page 299.

9. D. Martyn Lloyd-Jones *Preaching and Preachers* (London: Hodder and Stoughton 1985) page 97.

10. Dallas Willard, *Renovation of the Heart.*

Chapter 2

11. Ruben Exantus, '*Pastoral Burnout And Leadership Styles: Factors Contributing to Stress and Ministerial Turnover*' (Bloomington: Author House 2012) page 79.

12.   H. F. Lyte.

13.   Philip Graham Ryken, *Thomas Boston as Preacher of the Fourfold State* (Edinburgh: Rutherford House 1999), page 221–222.

14.   Ibid. page 57.

15.   John Calvin, *Institutes*, III.9.4–5. Tr. Henry Beveridge (London: James Clarke, 1949).

Chapter 3

16.   Thomas Boston, *Memoirs of Thomas Boston* (Edinburgh Banner of Truth 1988), page xi.

17.   Ibid. page 6.

18.   Ibid. pages 9–10.

19.   Ibid. page 137.

20.   Ibid. page 120.

21.   Ibid. page 37.

22.   H. J. Westing, *Church Staff Handbook* (Grand Rapids: Kregel Publications, 1997) page 43.

23.   Leland Ryken, *Worldly Saints* (Zondervan, 1986) page 220.

24.   Hermann N. Ridderbos, *The Gospel of John* (Cambridge: Eerdmans 1997) page 489.

25.   Thomas Boston, *Human Nature in its Fourfold State* (Edinburgh: Banner of Truth) page 478.

26.   Thomas Boston, *Human Nature in its Fourfold State,* page 506.

27.   Ibid. page 506.

28.   Oxford English Dictionary

29.   J. I. Packer, *Among God's Giants,* (Kingsway: Eastbourne, 1991) p.342.

30.   Ibid. p 24.

31.   Protestant Theological Seminary lecture

32.   Joel R. Beeke and Mark Jones, *A Puritan Theology: Doctrine For Life* (Grand Rapids: Reformation Heritage Books, 2012) page 843, Chapter 52 *Puritan Theology Shaped By A Pilgrim Mentality.* The footnote reads, 'I am indebted to an address

I heard by J. I. Packer decades ago for the basic framework of this chapter'. In it Joel Beeke outlines the same five features I am using here but with slightly different wording.

Chapter 4

33. Frank Allred, *Saints In Transit* (London: Grace Publications, 2010) page 97–98.

34. Thomas Boston, *Human Nature in its Fourfold State*, page 213.

35. Philip Ryken, *Thomas Boston as Preacher of the Fourfold State*, page 249.

36. Ibid. page 247.

37. C. S. Lewis, *The Lion, the witch and the wardrobe* (London: Harper Collins, 2009) page 195–6.

38. Paul Gardner, *Revelation: Focus on the Bible Series* (Fearn: Ross-shire Christian Focus, 2001) page 73.

39. Thomas Boston, *Human Nature in its Fourfold State,* page 434.

40. Ibid. page 442.

41. Ibid. page 444.

42. Ibid. page 455.

43. Ibid. page 459.

44. Charles Stanley, www.intouch.org.

Chapter 5

45. William Barclay, *Commentary on Hebrews* (Edinburgh: Saint Andrews Press, 1972) page 207.

46. J. C. Ryle, *Expository Thoughts on the Gospels: Matthew* (Welwyn: Evangelical Press, 1985), page 40.

47. Thomas Boston, *Memoirs of Thomas Boston,* page 81.

48. Dallas Willard, *Renovation of the Heart* (Leicester: IVP, 2002) page 24.

49. Ibid. page 25.

50. Ibid. page 21.

51. Ibid. page 23.

52. Ibid. page 25.

53. Leith Anderson quote is from unpublished notes by R. Daniel Reeves and Thomas Tumblin, 'Council on Ecclesiology: Preparation and Summaries' at Beeson Divinity School (Birmingham AL).

54. Thomas Boston, *Human Nature in its Fourfold State*, page 246.

55. Ibid. page 248.

56. Ibid. page 220.

57. W. E. Sangster, *Daily Readings* (London Epworth Press).

58. 'Why the Church Needs Saints, Part I' from W.E. Sangster, *The Pure in Heart: a Study in Christian Sanctity* (London: Epworth Press, 1954).

59. Ibid.

60. Dallas Willard, page 32.

61. Quoted in Katherine Makower, *The Coming of the Rain: the biography of a pioneering missionary in Rwanda* (Carlisle: Paternoster Press, 1999) page 93.

62. Thomas Boston, *Human Nature in its Fourfold State*, page 220.

63. Ibid.

64. Ibid.

Chapter 6

65. J. I. Packer, *Among God's Giants* (Kingsway: Eastbourne, 1991) page 44.

66. Leland Ryken, Worldly Saints, page 117.

67. http://www.fiec.org.uk/

68. Thomas Boston, *Human Nature in its Fourfold State*, page 223.

69. Ibid. page 224.

70. Ibid. page 232.

71. Melvyn Bragg, *The Book of Books* (London: Hodder and Stoughton, 2001) page 195.

72. David Bosch, *Transforming Mission* (New York: Orbis Books, 1991) page 390.

73. Chris Green, *The Message of the Church* (Nottingham: IVP, 2013) page 16.

Chapter 7

74. Martin Luther, *The Complete Sermons* (Grand Rapids: Baker, 2000) Volume 7, page 77.

75. Thomas Boston, *Human Nature in its Fourfold State*, page 206.

76. Ibid. page 208–209.

77. Ibid. page 209.

78. Ibid. 223–224.

79. Ibid. 224–225.

80. Ibid. 219.

81. http://thegospelcoalition.org/blogs/tgc/2014/01/03/what-i-wish-id-known-reflections-on-nearly-40-years-of-pastoral-ministry/ accessed 3/1/2014.

Chapter 8

82. Thomas Boston, *Memoirs of Thomas Boston,* page 35.

83. Ibid. page 44.

84. Ibid. page 54.

85. Ibid. page 64.

86. Ibid. page 69.

87. Ibid. page 107.

88. Ibid. page 111.

89. Ibid. page 118.

90. Ibid. page 124.

91. Ibid. page 137.

92. Ibid. page 149.

93. Ibid. page 155.

94. Ibid. page 157.

95. Ibid.

96. Ibid. page 475.

97. Ibid. page xxvi.

98. Ibid. page xxviii.

99.   John McKerrow, *History of the Secession Church* (Glasgow: Fullarton, 1841) page 20 Quoted by Philip Ryken page 42–43.

Chapter 9

100. J. I. Packer, *Among God's Giants,* p 24–25.

101. John Bunyan, *A Relation of My Imprisonment* (Edinburgh: Banner of Truth, 1991).

102. John Bunyan, *I will Pray with the Spirit* (c.1662) (Edinburgh: Banner of Truth, 1991).

103. John Bunyan, *A Confession of My Faith*, 1672, v. 191. (Edinburgh: Banner of Truth, 1991).

104. *Baptists in 17c century England* (Appendix of Oxford University Press Edition of *Grace Abounding*, 1998, page 225).

105. Lee Gatiss, *The Tragedy of 1662*, Location 285 London: Latimer Trust 2007.

106. Gary Brady, *1662 The Great Ejection* (Darlington: EP Books, 2012) page 157.

107. www.virtueonline.org.

108. http://www.virtueonline.org/portal/modules/news/article.php?storyid=12797.

109. Lee Gatiss, *The Tragedy of 1662*, Location 923.

110. Ibid. Location 886.

Chapter 10

111. All *Pilgrim's Progress* quotes from: John Bunyan, *Pilgrim's Progress* (Glasgow: Collins, 1953).

112. John Bunyan, *Grace Abounding* (Oxford University Press, 1998) page 89.

113. Ibid. page 89.

114. Gaius Davies, *Genius, Grief and Grace: A Doctor Looks At Suffering & Success* (Fearn, Ross-shire: Christian Focus, 2001) page 69.

115. Ibid. page 76.

116. Philip Edwards, 'The Journey in The Pilgrim's Progress,' *The Pilgrim's Progress, critical and Historical Views*, ed. Vincent Newey (Liverpool University Press 1980) p. 114.

117. John Bunyan, *Pilgrim's Progress* (Glasgow: Collins, 1953) page 170.

118. Ibid. page 173.

Chapter 11

119. http://www.logos.com/product/4218/the-practical-works-of-the-rev-richard-baxter#001.

120. Richard Baxter, *The Reformed Pastor* (Multnomah Press, 1982) page 68.

121. Ibid. page 85–86.

122. Ibid. page 116.

123. Ibid. page 35–36.

124. Ibid. page 41–42.

125. Ibid. page 11.

126. Ibid. page 47.

127. Ibid. pages 46–47.

128. Ibid. page 16.

129. Ibid. page 73.

130. Ibid. page 70.

131. Ibid. page 47.

132. Ibid. page 53.

133. Ibid. page 69.

Chapter 12

134. William Gurnall, *The Christian in Complete Armour*, Vol. I, Epistles Dedicatory (Edinburgh: Banner of Truth, 1995).

135. J. C. Ryle's introduction to *The Christian in Complete Armour*.

136. Ibid.

137. Gary Brady, *1662 The Great Ejection*, page 155.

138. http://en.wikiquote.org/wiki/Poland.

139. 'Conforming Puritan' Article reprinted from *Cross†Way*, Issue Spring 2012, No. 124.

140. Simon Ponsonby, *God is for us* (Grand Rapids: Monarch Books, 2013) page 25.

Chapter 13

141. John Bunyan, *The Heavenly Footman* (Fearn, Ross-shire: Christian Focus, 2002) page 50.

142. Ibid. page 52.

143. Simon Ponsonby, *God is For Us*, page 48.

144. John Bunyan, *The Heavenly Footman*, page 53–55.

145. Ibid. p. 55.

146. Ibid. pages 57–58.

147. Ibid. page 62.

148. Ibid. page 65.

149. Ibid. page 67.

150. Ibid. page 68.

151. Ibid. page 7.

Chapter 14

152. Richard Baxter, *The Saints' Everlasting Rest*, page 17.

153. Ibid. 255.

154. Calvin, *Institutes*, 3.9.4.

155. Richard Baxter, *The Saints' Everlasting Rest*, page 32.

156. Ibid. page 264.

157. Ibid. page 286.

158. Ibid. page 302.

159. Calvin, *Institutes*.

160. Ibid. 1.14.20.

161. Richard Baxter, *The Saints' Everlasting Rest* (Evangelical Press, 1978) page 245.

162. Ford Lewis Battles, *The Piety of John Calvin*, Calvin 500 series (Presbyterian and Reformed Publishing, 2009), pp. 111–112.

163. Calvin, *Institutes*, III.1.3.

164. Richard Baxter, *The Saints' Everlasting Rest*, page 261.

165. Richard Baxter, *The Saints' Everlasting Rest*, pages 260–263.

166. John Calvin, *On the Christian Life*, tr. Henry Beveridge [1845], at sacred-texts.com Chapter IV. 'Of Meditating on the eternal world'.

167. Gaius Davies, *Genius, Grief and Grace*, page 119.

168. Dietrich Bonhoeffer, *The Cost of Discipleship* (London: SCM Press, 2001) Memoir page xxiii.

169. Richard Baxter, *The Saints' Everlasting Rest*, page 301.

170. http://feedingonchrist.com/jesus-the-antitypical-sojourner-and-exile-in-a-foreign-land/

171. http://www.earlychristianwritings.com/text/diognetus-roberts.html *The Epistle of Mathetes to Diognetus* chapter V The Manner of Christians

Scripture Index